OCT 2 3 2006

W9-BEU-133

CULTURES OF THE WORLD®

MOROCCO

Pat Seward & Orin Hargraves

MARSHALL CAVENDISH BENCHMARK

NEW YORK

PICTURE CREDITS

Cover photo: © Peter Beck / Corbis
Bes Stock: 16, 76, 114 • Michael Brauner / Stockfood: 130 • Corbis, Inc.: 1, 50, 51, 53, 54, 92 • HBL
Network: 3, 4, 7, 8, 9, 11, 13, 18, 20, 23, 25, 26, 31, 37, 40, 43, 46, 48, 56, 57, 59, 60, 63, 64, 67, 73,
82, 84, 85, 86, 87, 90, 95, 96, 99, 100, 102, 108, 118, 119, 121, 123, 127, 128, 129 • Hulton Deutsch:
27 • Hutchison Library: 19, 21, 24, 28, 62, 117 • Richard I'Anson: 79, 104, 111 • International
Photobank: 14, 41, 44, 106 • John R. Jones: 6, 30, 80 • Jason Laure: 47, 58, 66, 98 • Lonely Planet
Images: 5, 49, 65, 124 • Barbara Lutterbeck / Stockfood: 131 • Christine Osborne: 10, 12, 15, 42, 68,
72, 75, 78, 81, 83, 89, 107, 112, 122 • T. Ozonas / Masterfile: 52 • Reuters: 32, 34 • Hans Rossel: 36,
120 • Pat Seward: 29, 38, 45, 61, 69, 70, 71, 77, 88, 94, 97, 101, 103, 105, 109, 110, 116, 126

PRECEDING PAGE
Two rural girls in the Moroccan desert.

Marshall Cavendish Benchmark
99 White Plains Road
Tarrytown, NY 10591
Website: www.marshallcavendish.us

© Times Editions Private Limited 1995
© Marshall Cavendish International (Asia) Private Limited 2006
All rights reserved. First edition 1995. Second edition 2006.
® "Cultures of the World" is a registered trademark of Times Publishing Limited.

Originated and designed by Times Editions
An imprint of Marshall Cavendish International (Asia) Private Limited
A member of Times Publishing Limited

All Internet sites were correct and accurate at the time of printing.

Library of Congress Cataloging-in-Publication Data
Seward, Pat, 1939–
   Morocco / Pat Seward, Orin Hargraves. – 2nd ed.
     p. cm. – (Cultures of the world)
   Includes bibliographical references and index.
   ISBN 0-7614-2051-7
   1. Morocco – Juvenile literature. I. Hargraves, Orin. II. Title. III. Series.
   DT305.S49 2006
   964 — dc22   2005020782

Printed in China

7 6 5 4 3 2 1

CONTENTS

INTRODUCTION 5

GEOGRAPHY 7
African mountains and Spanish enclaves • Coasts • Coastal plains and hinterland • Climate • Not enough water • A diversity of habitats • Animal life • Cities

HISTORY 19
Early days • Imperial Morocco • Arabs and Alaouites • Contacts with the outside world • The end of independence • Pacification not peace • Independence regained • A country to be reckoned with • The Green March

GOVERNMENT 31
Above all a kingdom • King and capital

ECONOMY 37
Privatization • Imports• Agriculture • Fishing • Mineral resources • Manufacturing • Tourism • The informal sector

ENVIRONMENT 49
Water • Something in the air • The earth versus the people

MOROCCANS 57
Population facts and figures • Berbers—the indigenous people • Arabs from the east • An Arab nation? • The real divide

LIFESTYLE 67
A different sense of time • Transportation • City life • French-style modern towns • Rural life • Wealth and work • Health • Education • The cornerstone of society • House and home • Women • Women's dress

A Moroccan artisan carefully paints a piece of furniture.

RELIGION   81
Islam in practice • Islam in Morocco • Saints and shrines
• The mosque • Medersas *and minarets • The Hassan II*
Mosque • Fès, city of minarets

LANGUAGE   93
Arabic Moroccan style • Berber languages • Other languages
• The media

ARTS   99
Architecture • Protecting oneself • Relaxation
• Carpets, kilims, *and silver • Music • Country style*

LEISURE   109
Entertainment Moroccan style • Traditional entertainment
• The sporting life • Soccer • Golfing the royal way

FESTIVALS   115
Religious celebrations and holidays • The Islamic calendar
• Moussem *merrymaking*

FOOD   121
Staples: bread and tajine *• The national dish • Olives*
and lemons • B'stilla *• Barbecued whole lamb • Pastries*
• In addition to tea • Eating in and eating out

MAP OF MOROCCO   132

ABOUT THE ECONOMY   135

ABOUT THE CULTURE   137

TIME LINE   138

GLOSSARY   140

FURTHER INFORMATION   141

BIBLIOGRAPHY   142

INDEX   142

A semi-nomad cooking in her tent.

INTRODUCTION

MOROCCO IS A LAND of geographic contrasts—landscapes of tranquil beauty and stark drama—and many social contradictions. It is an area with a long history and a sophisticated culture, yet it only became politically independent in 1956. It is, therefore, a young nation. For centuries it was isolated from the mainstream of world politics, but in the last 20 years it has begun to play a significant role in European, African, and Arab affairs.

With increasing polarization between Western and Muslim states, Morocco holds a significant position in world affairs as it is a moderate Muslim nation with significant ties to Europe and the United States. Although urban Morocco has a very European feel about it, centuries-old traditions still flourish and influence people's ideas and behavior. There are many tensions between rich and poor, traditionalist and modernist, pious and worldly. Yet outsiders recognize the presence of a moderate force in today's volatile and unpredictable world.

GEOGRAPHY

MOROCCO IS UNIQUE in many ways, not the least of which is its position as the African country closest to western Europe. The Mediterranean Sea runs along Morocco's northern border, with the port city of Tangier facing the southernmost point of Spain just across the Strait of Gibraltar.

The country's western border meets the Atlantic Ocean, while a large part of its eastern limit is a land border with Algeria. On this side, but farther south and west, Morocco's border is in dispute following Spain's withdrawal from its former colony of Rio d'Oro in the 1970s. This land, now generally known as Western Sahara, is claimed by Morocco. Legally, Morocco covers 172,413 square miles (446,300 square km). However, if Western Sahara is included, Morocco covers 274,461 square miles (710,850 square km).

Morocco is divided into five major areas: the Mediterranean coast, the Atlantic coast, the lowlands and plains, the Rif and Atlas mountain ranges, and the pre-Sahara.

In ancient mythology the Rock of Gibraltar and Jebel Musa (in Ceuta on the northernmost point of Morocco) were known as the Pillars of Hercules. The legend claims that they were formed when Hercules, one of the most celebrated heroes of Greek mythology, tore a mountain apart in order to get to Gades, modern Cádiz, on Spain's southwestern coast.

Left: **Melilla is a Spanish enclave surrounded by Moroccan land.**

Opposite: **Berber tribesmen at the sand dunes of Erg Chebbi near Merzouga. Close to 50 percent of Morocco is desert.**

Various stories attempt to explain how the Atlas Mountains got their name. Perhaps the most prevalent myth is that of Atlas, who supported the pillars separating heaven and earth. The Greeks believed these pillars rested in the sea somewhere beyond their western horizon. Over the passage of many centuries, the name Atlas was transferred to the peaks of the westernmost mountains of North Africa, which were seen as supporting the sky above.

AFRICAN MOUNTAINS AND SPANISH ENCLAVES

In the north the Rif Mountains run along the Mediterranean coast, rising steeply from the sea to heights of more than 8,000 feet (2,454 m). Farther south are three separate mountain chains that cross the country diagonally. They divide the fertile coastal plains from the Sahara Desert.

The most northerly of the three is the Middle Atlas, which overlooks the plain south of the foothills of the Rif. A narrow gap in this range offers the only reasonably easy land route between western Algeria and the Atlantic Ocean. Much of the range consists of a limestone plateau dissected by river gorges and punctuated by volcanic craters. It is also flanked by two rivers: the Sebou flowing into the Atlantic and the Moulouya flowing into the Mediterranean.

To the south the Middle Atlas merges with the High Atlas—the central, most formidable, and highest of the three ranges. Many a peak here rises to 12,000 feet (3,657 m), and snow-clad summits are seen in winter.

The most southerly range, the Anti-Atlas, is the shortest, lowest, and most sparsely populated of the three. Its barren southern slopes are slashed by many gorges but softened by the green of cultivated palm groves. Beyond are the endless wastes of the Sahara sands.

There are scarcely any easy routes across the High Atlas, but the numerous mountain tracks are well used by the local population living in the mountain valleys, often in compact fortified villages.

CEUTA AND MELILLA

In the 1970s Spain relinquished its claims to its Rio d'Oro colony south of Morocco. However, it still retains two enclaves—tiny patches of Spanish soil surrounded by Moroccan territory—at Ceuta on the Mediterranean coast close to Tangier and at Melilla near the Algerian border. These are remnants of history in the same way that Britain still retains Gibraltar on Spain's southern coast.

Both enclaves have long histories going back to Phoenician and Roman times. Today Spain rejects Morocco's territorial claim over Ceuta and Melilla, and the Spanish legislature is currently considering granting autonomous status to these two enclaves.

COASTS

Morocco is bounded by the sea on two sides. The Mediterranean coast is a mixture of sandy and rugged beaches, backed by cliffs and sandwiched between rocky inlets and headlands. Swimming is relatively safe, and the scenery is often dramatic. For these reasons, the area is becoming increasingly popular with tourists. Tourism is one of the country's fastest-growing industries and is vital to the economy for the jobs it creates and the much-needed foreign exchange it generates.

The Atlantic coast near Tan-Tan.

Morocco's Mediterranean coast is still generally unspoiled. Tétouan at the western end is a beautiful town with a long history. Several small resorts are nearby. Al Hoceima, halfway along the coast, is the area's main resort. Oujda, one of Morocco's largest cities, is on the Algerian border at the eastern end of the coastal region.

In contrast to the Mediterranean, vast stretches of sandy beach washed by long Atlantic waves characterize the country's western coast. As on the northern coast there are many lively seaside towns and a few major vacation resorts. In particular Agadir in the south is a winter playground for sun-starved northern Europeans. In addition to new resorts there are several old cities, such as Asilah, Al-Jadida, and Essaouira.

Morocco has around 21 ports of some importance. Of its eight international ports, six—Tangier, Kénitra, Mohammedia, Casablanca, Safi, and Agadir—are situated along the Atlantic coast.

COASTAL PLAINS AND HINTERLAND

Stretching inland from the coast is an extensive area of lowland enclosed to the north by the Rif Mountains and to the east and south by the Middle and High Atlas ranges. These coastal and inland plains are Morocco's most densely populated areas. The country's major cities—Casablanca, the commercial capital; Rabat, the political capital; Marrakech; and Fès—are located either on the Atlantic coast or in the fertile lowland plains.

Across the barrier of the Atlas Mountains, to the east and south, Morocco is a land of arid plateaus and, especially in the northeast, of rocky tablelands, towering ravines, and fortified villages set in green oases. Towns here are situated on the edge of the Sahara. Er Rachidia is a bustling and prosperous market. Erfoud is the last major stop before the sand dunes begin at Merzouga. Ouarzazate and the surrounding areas rose to fame as locations for various desert film epics. Farther west is the walled city of Taroudant. Beyond these isolated oases of civilization lie the vast expanses of the Sahara. In this great emptiness, nevertheless, there are treasures—valuable minerals such as phosphates and possibly oil—that fuel the ongoing disputes over Western Sahara.

Morocco has a coastline that extends for 1,140 miles (1,835 km), and Moroccan waters contain some of the world's richest fisheries.

CLIMATE

Morocco has been described as "a cold country with a hot sun." In fact its climate, although undeniably hot in summer, is extremely varied, and some regions can be quite cold. Moroccans living near the northern coast enjoy Mediterranean conditions. Farther south there is both greater heat and greater humidity in semitropical areas. Inland, people have to cope with greater extremes and more sudden variations in temperature, whereas to the south and east the pre-Sahara and the desert proper are subject to desert conditions—scorching hot temperatures by day and biting cold at night.

The upper elevations of the High Atlas range are snow-covered from November through April.

The lands north and west of the Atlas Mountains, including the Rif Mountains, are subject to cool, wet winters and dry, moderately hot summers. Conditions vary according to latitude and altitude as well as proximity to the Atlantic coast where sea breezes lessen the summer heat. Southerly coastal areas can be humid but can also be intensely hot if, as occasionally happens, arid winds blow up from the Sahara and dry out the lowlands.

Mountain dwellers endure hard, cold winters with heavy snowfall in the highest altitudes and pleasantly warm summers. Lowlands away from the coasts tend to be hot and stifling in summer and unpleasantly cold and damp in winter. In the rest of the country the climate becomes progressively more arid and extreme the farther east and south one goes.

The dunes of Tinfou in the Sahara Desert.

Drought is one of Morocco's biggest problems. If rainfall was more frequent and rainfall patterns more reliable, the country's agricultural potential could be better exploited. In the 1980s and 1990s insufficient rain severely affected agricultural production on otherwise fertile land and caused many economic and social problems.

NOT ENOUGH WATER

In the Rif Mountains and northern parts of the Middle Atlas, rainfall averages more than 29 inches (74 cm) per year. In other parts of the Middle Atlas, in the High Atlas, and in the northern half of the Atlantic lowlands, average rainfall is between 15 and 29 inches (38 and 74 cm) per year. Farther south, in the southern lowlands and the Anti-Atlas, rain becomes scant—between 8 and 15 inches (20 and 38 cm)—and also more variable, insufficient for the cultivation of grain crops without irrigation. East and south of the Atlas Mountains, rainfall is even scarcer and more unpredictable. The Sahara areas might receive as little as 4 inches (10 cm) of rain annually.

SELECTED AVERAGE TEMPERATURES

Ouarzazate (in the pre-Sahara):
Summer 104°F (39°C)
Winter 34°F (1°C)

Tangier (on the Mediterranean coast):
Summer 80°F (26°C)
Winter 46°F (8°C)

Ketama (in the Rif Mountains):
Summer 80°F (26°C)
Winter 30°F (-1°C)

Casablanca (on the Atlantic coast):
Summer 78°F (25°C)
Winter 44°F (6°C)

ANCIENT ANIMALS

Ancient rock carvings in the south and mosaics dating from the first two centuries A.D. at the Roman city of Volubilis in the north reveal a countryside and a climate somewhat different from those of today. The land around Volubilis is some of the most fertile in North Africa. It supplied the Roman Empire with wheat and olive oil, as well as lions and other wild beasts for the infamous Roman "games." In addition to lions, there were bears and elephants and, farther south, ostriches and antelope—animals only seen today in the protected confines of wildlife parks.

The Roman thirst for bloodshed as entertainment, a deteriorating climate, and prolonged and relentless hunting in more modern times have combined to deprive Morocco of many species of animals. A few lions survived in the Middle Atlas ranges until the 1920s, but the elephants that were once said to inhabit the area around Rabat on the Atlantic coast are gone forever. So, too, are the ostrich, the bubal hartebeest, and several other large mammals.

A DIVERSITY OF HABITATS

Climatic changes have affected Morocco's natural flora, and the country has a unique diversity of habitats, each with its indigenous species. At one end of the scale are the arid mountain deserts and endless expanses of Sahara sands, and at the other, equally arid areas of perpetual snow on the peaks of the highest mountains. In between these extremes lie fertile valleys and coastal plains blessed with temperatures and rainfall that vary from a typically Mediterranean climate to a typically subtropical climate.

The plains and lowlands abound in colorful Mediterranean plants and support many varieties of fruits, vegetables, and grains. Row upon row of olive trees grow in straight lines across the plains, and in many places vast tracts of nonindigenous eucalyptus have transformed the landscape. The slopes of the mountain ranges are well wooded with evergreen oak at lower levels and giant, sweet-smelling cedar higher up.

Storks nesting in the center of a town.

14

East and south of the Atlas Mountains, the lowlands are dominated by scrubby steppe and desert vegetation—aromatic herbs, stunted trees and bushes, and most importantly, the ubiquitous date palm. The desert fringes are marked by patches of coarse grass, varieties of thistles, and cacti.

ANIMAL LIFE

As one would expect, reptiles are fairly widespread. Lizards, chameleons, geckos, and snakes are common, and the desert is home to the fascinating sand fish—the well-camouflaged, yellow-brown Berber skink that appears to "swim" through the sand.

Mammals, especially the larger species, are relatively rare. The most common large animals are sheep, goats, and camels, which are able to survive in generally inaccessible and virtually barren land. Red foxes are also occasionally seen, and a type of monkey known as the Barbary ape frequents the cedar forests. Wild boar are plentiful, and shooting them is a popular sport.

The desert fringes are inhabited by many smaller mammals such as the sand squirrel, which lives on hot rock faces, and gazelle and antelope, which graze the thorn bushes and dry grasses. The desert proper is inhabited by animals like the jerboa, the desert fox, and the desert hedgehog.

Date palms.

CITIES

Almost without exception, Morocco's most populous cities are located in the western lowland areas of the country. Casablanca and Rabat-Salé are on the Atlantic coast; Fès and Marrakech are farther inland. However, Oujda, Morocco's fifth largest city, is located in the east, on an important trading crossroads—the border with Algeria.

Casablanca is the country's commercial and industrial capital.

Casablanca, Morocco's largest city and the third largest city in North Africa after Cairo and Alexandria, is the country's commercial capital. Next in order of size are three of the four "imperial cities"—Marrakech, Rabat-Salé, and Fès. Meknès, the last of these four, is considerably smaller.

At one time or another each of the four imperial cities served as a capital, but with the exception of Rabat, they were not capitals of Morocco as we know it today. Rather they served as the power base of one of the many groups who held power after the arrival of the Arabs from the east in the late seventh century.

Fès, the oldest of the four, was founded toward the end of the eighth century and quickly became a religious and educational center. It lies in the heart of a fertile basin between the Middle Atlas and Rif mountains and at the crossroads of two important

PRINCIPAL CITIES AND TOWNS

Here are estimated population figures for Morocco's major towns and cities in 2005. There is continuous migration from the countryside to the urban areas, and population figures quickly become out of date.

Casablanca	3,462,648
Agadir	2,005,703
Rabat	1,889,635
Fès	1,223,087
Marrakech	969,420
Tangier	851,321
Meknès	587,315
Oujda	456,523
Kenitra	428,181
Tétouan	368,485
Safi	335,164

In their heyday the four imperial cities were political, religious, and cultural centers. Today they contain the majority of Morocco's treasured historical and cultural monuments.

trade routes: one across the Sahara to central Africa, the other eastward toward the rest of North Africa.

Next in terms of age is Meknès, which is located near Fès. Despite being founded in the 10th century, it did not achieve any real importance until the 17th century, when it became the capital under Sultan Moulay Ismail, ancestor of the current king, Mohammed VI.

Similarly, Rabat has a long history. Although an important city from the 12th century onward, Rabat did not become a capital, and then only briefly, until the second half of the 18th century. In the 20th century, when the French were empowered to "protect" Morocco, it became their administrative center. Since independence, Rabat has remained the capital of modern Morocco.

The history of Marrakech, to the north of the High Atlas range, goes back to 1062. It probably started life as a town of tents around a *kasbah* (KAHS-bah), or fortress, in a vast palm grove but quickly became the heart of an empire stretching from Catalonia in eastern Spain to the mountains of medieval Sudan. Its fortunes rose and fell as successive dynasties also rose and fell. Today it is still sometimes called the capital of the "great south."

HISTORY

NO ONE KNOWS FOR SURE, but it seems likely that about 1 million years ago ancestors of the human species—groups of hunter-gatherer hominids—roamed the empty spaces of North Africa. What is certain is that the North Africa of prehistoric times was quite different from the North Africa of today. Prehistoric North Africa was probably an area of dense forests and fertile plains that supported a wide range of wild game such as elephant, zebra, lion, giraffe, ostrich, and antelope. Changes in climate beginning around 3000 B.C. produced the arid lands of the north and the Sahara Desert of today.

Neanderthals lived in Morocco about 50,000 years ago, and remains from this period, such as a young man around 16 years old, were discovered near Rabat in 1933. "Rabat man" and his relatives were followed by Stone Age humans, who established primitive pastoral and agricultural systems in the last 10,000 years B.C.

By the time of recorded history, the area was inhabited by light-skinned tribal peoples who probably had Euro-Asiatic origins and came to be known as Berbers. Little by little the Berber tribes spread across the whole of North Africa and are now recognized as the indigenous people of Morocco. From about the sixth or seventh centuries B.C. onward, they came into brief contact first with Phoenicians, then with Carthaginians, and finally with Romans. All three groups arrived in small numbers, and none had any long-term impact.

These fleeting visitors, however, were followed in the seventh century by Arab immigrants from much farther east. They too came in small numbers, but they brought with them a culture and a religion that transformed the country into the Arab state and Muslim society that it is today.

Above: **A prehistoric rock painting of a gazelle.**

Opposite: **Ruins of the basilica at Volubilis date from Roman times.**

19

EARLY DAYS

The first outsiders to establish a foothold in Berber Morocco were Phoenicians from the eastern Mediterranean. They were a maritime people and their main objective was the creation of trading settlements along the northern coast of the continent where they could set up facilities to salt fish. Carthage, in modern Tunisia, was the main focus of their interest, and they made little significant contact with the inhabitants of the Moroccan interior.

When Carthage itself became an independent state, Carthaginian traders developed the existing Phoenician settlements into prosperous towns with fish salting and preserving as major industries. They also grew wheat and grapes, and minted coins. Unlike their predecessors, the Carthaginians exercised some cultural influence over the Berbers and penetrated inland, at least as far as the region around Volubilis between the Rif and Middle Atlas mountains.

The Carthaginian Empire went into decline in the face of growing Roman expansion, culminating in the sacking of Carthage in 146 B.C. In due course the Romans took over Carthaginian outposts in Morocco and incorporated them into two large provinces. But

A Volubilis mosaic.

the newcomers found themselves embroiled in constant conflict with Berber tribes. One rebellion took three years and 20,000 troops to subdue.

Although the Romans did not expand much farther south, they exploited the fertile vineyards and grainfields they had inherited and built aqueducts and reservoirs to bring water into drought-ridden areas. Streets and private

buildings, numerous sculptures and other decorations, well-preserved mosaics, and items essential to daily life, such as sundials and cooking utensils, have survived. Together they present a remarkable record of the wealth of the inhabitants and the life of the times.

After 300 years of dealing with uprisings, and faced with declining productivity, the Romans eventually moved their administrative centers farther east. Shortly after the middle of the third century, they left Morocco for good and the country entered a dark age about which little is known. Life presumably went on much as before, and the coastal regions were disturbed only by the occasional incursion of Vandals and Goths sweeping south from Spain en route to northern Tunisia. For a brief period parts of the coast were also incorporated into the Byzantine Empire.

This situation came to an end around 680 with the arrival of a wave of dynamic new invaders. These battle-hardened pioneers from the Arabian peninsula spread across North Africa when their expansion in other directions was temporarily blocked. Land and conquest aside, their principal aim was to convert the world to Islam, the new religion they brought from the east. A longer-term objective was to use Morocco as a springboard for the invasion and conversion of Spain.

Roman imperial roads reached across France and Spain, and then down from Tangier, until they finally stopped at Volubilis, the empire's most remote base. The city occupied a dramatic site on a long, high plateau above a river valley. It was encircled by ramparts with six gates. One gate and several fragments of the walls still remain, along with large parts of the main buildings—the capitol, the basilica, and the triumphal arch.

21

IMPERIAL MOROCCO

Moroccan history before independence is largely a saga of shifting alliances, sporadic bids for power, and the rise and fall of various dynasties, some Arab and some with a Berber tribal basis.

Beginning in the eighth century, a succession of Moroccan ruling sultans controlled the plains, the coastal ports, and the areas around Fès, Marrakech, Rabat, and Meknès—the so-called imperial cities. Outside these cities, the inhabitants of the Rif and Atlas ranges and the remote deserts seldom recognized any authority beyond that of the local tribal head.

The first group to gain substantial power were the Idrissids, led by Moulay Idriss who reached Morocco in the late eighth century. He succeeded in converting many Berbers to Islam and gained enough control, at least in the north, to set up an Arab court and kingdom.

The Idrissid dynasty was short-lived and was ousted in the 11th century by Muslim Berber rulers called the Almoravids, who moved in to rescue Moroccan Islam from the decadent habits into which they felt it had fallen. They also founded Marrakech.

When the power of the Almoravids waned, they were replaced by another Berber dynasty, the Almohads, an intensely puritanical group similarly bent on religious reform. Their most noteworthy sultan was Yacoub el Mansour, who ruled from Rabat.

MEKNÈS—THE VERSAILLES OF MOROCCO

Moulay Ismail, the second Alaouite sultan, made Meknès his capital for the 55 years of his notorious reign (1672–1727). The most tyrannical of all Moroccan rulers, he was feared for his appalling cruelty, but revered for his devotion to Islam and for bringing peace and prosperity after a period of anarchy.

He was also an enthusiastic builder and created Meknès to rival the palace of Versailles in France. In its heyday the city boasted numerous mosques and bazaars, 50 palaces, 16 miles (25.75 km) of exterior walls pierced by 20 gates, and enormous granaries to store food for his 12,000 horses.

ARABS AND ALAOUITES

The Almohads were followed by another two successive Berber dynasties and finally, in the 16th century, by the second Arab dynasty, the Saadians, who established their base in Marrakech. The Saadians rose to power solely on the strength of their position as descendants of the Prophet Mohammed, and their dynasty was important because it was the first whose power did not depend on tribal alliances.

In the 17th century, when civil war erupted among rival heirs, the Saadians were ousted by the Alaouites, another Arab dynasty. They, too, suffered from family strife, civil war, and rebellion. As the centuries passed, these problems were compounded by outdated forms of government, bankruptcy, and widespread discontent.

This situation left the way open for increasing intervention by foreigners and finally European occupation. By the early years of the 20th century, "imperial" Morocco was a thing of the past; tribal power had once again replaced centralized control in the Moroccan interior.

The mausoleum of Moulay Ismail at Meknes.

CONTACTS WITH THE OUTSIDE WORLD

The first Arabs arrived in Morocco in the late seventh century. They were followed at intervals by succeeding waves of Arab invaders similarly bent on conquest and conversion of the Berbers. Thereafter the increasingly mixed Arab-Berber population fiercely guarded their independence in the face of growing European interest in the territory. Initially most contact was with Spain and Portugal, and various settlements on the Moroccan coasts changed hands many times from the 15th century onward. Moroccan involvement in European politics varied according to the situation at home. At one time dissident Moroccans sought the help of Portuguese armies to settle their own quarrels. On the other hand, in the 17th century, the Alaouite sultan Moulay Ismail felt powerful enough to contemplate marriage with a French princess. The French ridiculed the idea.

From the end of the Napoleonic Wars onward, Morocco fought a losing battle against European ambitions.

THE END OF INDEPENDENCE

In the last decades of the 18th century, with weak rulers and strife at home, Morocco became isolated until Europeans began to take a more consistent interest in their closest African neighbor. In the first half of the 19th century, the French occupied territory in neighboring Algeria and inflicted a severe defeat on the Moroccan sultan when he went to the assistance of his fellow Muslims. A few years later Spain acquired

TANGIER, THE "INTERNATIONAL" CITY

Tangier—Morocco's sixth largest city—is the country's most cosmopolitan, atypical, and internationally famous metropolis. It is steeped in legend and its history involves interaction with Phoenicians, Carthaginians, Romans, Portuguese, and Spanish. It was even a British possession for a short period at the end of the 17th century. At the beginning of the 20th century, the city was designated an international port so that no one power would have absolute control. The arrangement was enthusiastically promoted by the British, who wished to prevent Spain from controlling both sides of the Strait of Gibraltar.

Sidi Ifni on Morocco's Atlantic coast. By the end of the century, Morocco was virtually bankrupt due to an unstable, insular economy, and Spain and France used every opportunity to interfere in domestic affairs on the pretext of "protecting" their own citizens working in Morocco. Last-minute attempts at reform, which might have saved Morocco by modernizing its antiquated forms of government, failed miserably.

Meanwhile Britain, France, Germany, Spain, and Italy vied with one another to gain possession of the last few remnants of independent Africa. The European powers negotiated "spheres of influence" among themselves. Eventually France and Spain, made a secret agreement about how they would divide up Morocco when circumstances permitted.

In 1908, Moroccans revolted against the increasing influence of the "infidels" in their land. While the sultan was occupied with this emergency, Spain moved 90,000 troops into Melilla, claiming that they were there to protect Spanish workers employed in mining. This event marked the start of foreign occupation. Unable to assert his authority and presiding over a debt-ridden nation, in 1912 Sultan Hafid signed the Treaty of Fès, which officially brought Morocco under French and Spanish "protection." Under the treaty most of Morocco was taken over by the French, and the Spanish received parts of its northern coast. The Protectorates lasted 44 years.

The process of European advance, once started, was impossible to stop. Internal rebellions and revolts weakened Moroccan rulers and made it easier for Europeans to establish footholds on Moroccan soil.

The Spanish fort of Al Hoceima. The Spanish presence in Morocco was much less beneficial than the French. Their policies tended to provoke rebellion rather than bring peace and were instrumental in turning armed revolt into middle-class resistance.

Direct French administration sidelined the traditional ruling classes, and it is said that the sultan had to read French newspapers to find out what was going on in his own country.

PACIFICATION NOT PEACE

Under the terms of the Protectorate agreements, France became the dominant power in Morocco and took over what it called "useful Morocco"—the main cities on the central plains and all the territory along the Algerian border. Spain was granted two strips of territory (one along the northern coast and the other in the south, running eastward from Tarfaya), the enclave of Sidi Ifni, and parts of the Sahara Desert.

At first the terms of the Protectorate Treaty were scrupulously observed by General Lyautey, the first French Resident-General. Succeeding administrators, however, turned Morocco into a French colony in all but name. Nevertheless the French presence imposed much-needed stability, and little by little tribal rebellion was subdued. By 1934 the whole of French Morocco was under effective central control.

From the Moroccan point of view the French Protectorate had both advantages and disadvantages. Peace brought a flood of French settlers who took over the best land but also developed it in a way that had not been possible before. Roads and railways opened up the country, new towns were built, the administration was modernized, the legal system was reformed, and education became more widely available. However, ambitious, educated young Moroccans had few outlets for their talents.

INDEPENDENCE REGAINED

Nationalist sentiment began to make itself felt in the 1930s with the formation of the Istiqlal (Freedom) Party. French attempts to divide and rule by driving a wedge between Arabs and Berbers had the opposite effect—the two groups united in common opposition.

The French made Mohammed V sultan at the age of 17 in the hope that he would be easily controlled. However in public speeches the young sultan spoke about the rights of the Moroccan people and their history of independence. He also signed the demand for reforms submitted by nationalist leaders.

The sultan paralyzed the government by refusing to sign legislation limiting his power, and in desperation, as rioting began, the French exiled him to Madagascar. He went quietly but refused to abdicate, an astute move that increased his popularity and stimulated nationalist fervor and spiraling violence. In November 1955 Mohammed V was allowed to return. In March of the following year the Protectorate period came to an end. Morocco was independent once more.

Mohammed V attending a festival the year before his death in 1961. His son, Hassan, the father of the present king of Morocco, leads his horse.

GENERAL HUBERT GONZALVE LYAUTEY

Lyautey, the first French Resident-General, grew to love the country he was sent to pacify and "protect." His aim was to avoid destroying age-old Moroccan traditions and habits and to take all action in the name and with the consent of the sultan and the traditional Moroccan elite.

His policy of building new, modern towns outside the ancient cities meant that the old *medinas*, or native towns, were left untouched and Moroccan lifestyle, as far as possible, was preserved. He was scrupulously careful not to undermine Islam or destroy any of its monuments.

Sahrawi riders in the Western Sahara. The bid for independence in Western Sahara continues in spite of Moroccan claims to the territory.

Young professionals eager to press ahead with modernizing reforms feel frustrated by the conservative policies of the "old guard" who fought for independence.

A COUNTRY TO BE RECKONED WITH

As a modern nation, Morocco is just about 50 years old. In the short period since it regained independence, its people have had to tackle problems that older nations have had generations to address. The French left behind a well-developed industrial sector, the beginnings of a good irrigation system, and a network of roads and railways, at least in "useful Morocco." Yet they also left many problems: a political system that would prove difficult to transform into an independent modern government, a lack of trained Moroccan administrators, and an abundance of ethnic and regional divisions fueled by the protracted struggle for independence.

Nonetheless, more regions are now being developed and modest health and educational facilities are being put in place. Agriculture and industry have diversified, but widespread poverty hampers progress. Morocco is still heavily in debt and in need of foreign investment.

To the outsider the numerous attempts to dethrone or assassinate King Hassan II, Morocco's second monarch and son of Mohammed V, were signs of instability in the country. But Hassan ruled until his death in 1999, and the transition of leadership to his son, the now-reigning

Mohammed VI, was smooth and widely accepted. Mohammed VI is regarded as the king who will bring Morocco into the 21st century with skill and confidence. Life is an uphill struggle for the vast majority of Moroccans, but they are slowly forging a nation that is beginning to take its place in the modern world.

THE GREEN MARCH

The issue of Western Sahara has bedeviled North African politics since the 1960s, when valuable phosphate deposits were discovered there. The inhabitants of the territory called for decolonization from Spain, and then for independence. After more than 40 years, the question is unresolved.

Morocco lays claim to the territory. It argues that the Saharan tribal leaders traditionally acknowledged the authority of the Moroccan sultans, but the International Court of Justice has ruled that this is not sufficient to establish sovereignty. In November 1975, in the so called Green March, 350,000 Moroccan citizens walked into the Western Saharan area in support of Morocco's claim. Moroccans in the area now outnumber the original inhabitants by three to two. Meanwhile arguments continue about who should be eligible to take part in a United Nations sponsored referendum to decide the future of the territory. Morocco has built hundreds of miles of defenses to secure the border, although 75 countries now recognize the Polisario's Sahrawi Arab Democratic Republic as the legitimate government of Western Sahara.

A stamp commemorating the Green March. In the eyes of the ordinary Moroccan, the Western Sahara conflict is a cause behind which the nation can unite.

29

GOVERNMENT

THE KINGDOM OF MOROCCO is a constitutional monarchy and a Muslim state with limited democratic aspects. As a monarchy, it enjoys the distinction of being the oldest of its kind in the Muslim world. King Mohammed VI is a member of the Alaouite dynasty, which has been in power for most of the last 300 years.

Morocco has a bicameral parliament, in which one house is popularly elected; but it does not have legislative authority over all aspects of government. Nothing official happens in Morocco without the king's explicit sanction. The current king has made greater advances toward democracy than his predecessors, but Morocco today is a very long way from anything that would seem democratic to western Europe or North America.

Local government is broken down by regions, of which there are 16, including those in Western Sahara, which Morocco effectively administers. Each region has a governor; the regions are in turn divided into more than 1,500 urban and rural communes under officials known as *pashas* and *caids* (KAA-eeds). The legal system is based on Islamic law and the French and Spanish civil law systems left over from colonial days.

The lack of full democracy and the feeling that the judicial system is slow, erratic, and, in some cases, corrupt fuels a simmering discontent, especially among educated young Moroccans. However, by comparison with some other Arab or African countries, Morocco has a livelier and more diversified political life, although issues such as the role of the monarchy, Morocco's status as a Muslim country, and the policy on the disputed Western Sahara are not open to discussion.

Morocco, Tunisia, and Algeria are known collectively in the Arab world as Jeziret al-Maghreb, or Island of the West. Morocco's Arabic name is El Maghreb el Aqsa, meaning "the farthest west."

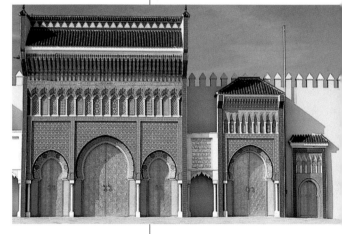

Above: **The Royal Palace in Fès.**

Opposite: **A guard at the Mohammed V mausoleum.**

ABOVE ALL A KINGDOM

The Polisario Front has been fighting for the independence of the Western Sahara. The United Nations is currently attempting to negotiate a referendum on the status of the Western Sahara.

In spite of the wording of the constitution, Morocco is more accurately described as an absolute monarchy than as a democratic state. Ever since independence was restored in 1956 it has been governed by a sovereign with extensive powers to manipulate a weak parliamentary system.

Morocco has a bicameral parliament. The upper house, or Chamber of Counselors, has 270 seats, and its members are elected indirectly by local councils, professional organizations, and labor syndicates for nine-year terms. One-third of the members are up for election every three years. The lower house is the Chamber of Representatives. It has 325 seats; 295 of its members are elected by multi-seat constituencies and 30 from national lists of women. Its members are elected by popular vote for six-year terms.

For most of Morocco's post-independence history, the bulk of the power resided with the right wing and the center groups, which together are often described as the loyalist parties, with the smaller left-wing and other groups forming the opposition. Since 1998, however, left-wing parties have won enough parliamentary seats in elections to form coalition governments. Yet, to date,

no single party has so far achieved the clear majority required to control the parliament, and Moroccans in general have accepted the need for a strong unifying central power in order to ensure stability. This acceptance of centralized power has its roots in traditional forms of government in the past and enables the monarchy to retain substantial control of both foreign and domestic policy.

The pattern of centralized control is repeated at the local level. Each of the regions has an elected assembly, but the real power lies in the hands of the governor, who is appointed by the Ministry of the Interior.

THE PATH TO DEMOCRACY

Dissent is fueled by the frustrated aspirations of educated young Moroccans, widespread poverty, high unemployment, poor education, inadequate health services, and lack of housing. Criticisms, which include sporadic allegations of corruption, and charges that Morocco has been an absolute monarchy for the last 20 to 30 years, have often been met with severe reprimand at best and imprisonment at worst. On occasion striking workers have been jailed. Nevertheless the signs are that Morocco is slowly advancing toward a more representative government that can implement its own policies.

The greatest hope for democratic reform in modern Morocco is seen in actions taken by King Mohammed VI. Shortly after he ascended the throne he freed many political prisoners who had languished in miserable conditions for decades. Then, in January 2004, the king appointed a former political prisoner, Driss Benzekri, to head the newly formed Justice and Reconciliation Commission. This 16-member commission is made up of experts on human rights, as well as nationally recognized figures from the fields of law, medicine, and women's rights. Among them are other former political prisoners and victims of torture. In contrast, however, the Moroccan government has been ruthless in its suppression of fundamentalist Islam and any group that is thought to have links with international terrorism. Many critics feel that measures adopted in the wake of the 2003 bomb attacks in Casablanca have canceled any gains made in human rights.

KING AND CAPITAL

Since independence, Morocco has had three monarchs: Mohammed V, his son Hassan II (who reigned from 1961 to his death in 1999), and Hassan's son Mohammed VI. The king plays a dual role as both spiritual and secular head of state.

King Mohammed VI addresses foreign dignitaries at the Royal Palace in Marrakech.

The king's spiritual title translates as "Commander of the Faithful." It stems from the royal family's claim of descent from the Prophet Mohammed, a distinction that makes the family sacred in the eyes of Muslim Moroccans. Any challenge to their authority would be a challenge to their divine right to rule, and very few in Morocco are willing to be perceived as questioning this authority: it would be seen as a challenge to Islam, which followers regard as the perfect (i.e., ultimate and unassailable) religion. As long as Morocco's most pressing problems are being addressed, however slowly, the authority of the king will probably be accepted.

As the secular head of state, the king is firmly in control of domestic and foreign policy. The current king has the benefit of a liberal education, much of it obtained in Europe, and many regard him as a capable leader for a modern Muslim state. He inherited from his father the allegiance of the vast majority of Moroccans, who came to see the monarchy as a suitable symbol for their country during the late king's reign. The challenges for the current monarch are many. He cannot afford to alienate the very strong Islamic element that is one of the pillars of his support, but at the same time he must distance himself from the extremists of Islam who favor isolation from the West, rather than dialogue. At the same time, he is determined to modernize the infrastructure of Morocco so that it might one day be feasible to realize the country's ultimate goal: integration into the European Union.

Morocco's capital is Rabat, one of the four ancient imperial cities. It is the chief residence of the monarch and the seat of government. The city acquired its name in the 10th century A.D. when it became a military garrison, or *ribat* (ree-BAT), meaning fortified camp.

Rabat is an elegant, busy city with two faces. On one hand, it has the broad avenues and abundant trees and flowers of the modern administrative center established by the French during the Protectorate period. On the other hand, it has the narrow, whitewashed streets of the older town that goes back possibly to medieval times.

Today the heart of modern Rabat lies in the great open grounds and many courtyards of the *Mechouar* (mesh-WAAR), or royal enclosure, with its wealth of modern Moroccan decorative architecture. The royal palace, the royal mosque, the offices of the prime minister, the Supreme Court of Justice, and various ministries are all located here.

After Morocco regained independence, Mohammed V changed his title from sultan to king in order to demonstrate his intention of ruling along progressive lines.

THE NATIONAL FLAG

Morocco's national flag features a five-pointed star, called the Seal of Sulayman (Solomon), in the center of a plain red background. Red flags with various emblems have long been used by members of the Alouites, the dynasty that has ruled Morocco since the 17th century. The green Seal of Sulayman was added in 1915 during the time of the French Protectorate.

ECONOMY

MOROCCO DOES NOT have the good fortune to be part of the oil-rich Arab world. This means that it has to spend quite heavily on fuel for its energy needs. On the other hand, it has enormous phosphate deposits and a climate that, along with land and water resources, has allowed for the development of an agricultural sector that plays a vital role in both the domestic and export markets. The manufacturing sector contributes about 30 percent to the gross domestic product (GDP), and the services sector includes a dynamic tourism industry.

Over 60 percent of Morocco's exports go to the European Union. France receives the largest proportion with 33.6 percent of the total, followed by Spain with 17.4 percent. Other important trading partners include the United Kingdom, Italy, and Germany. The United States imports about 4 percent of Morocco's products.

The economy is expanding; growth rates were usually between 4 and 4.5 percent during the 1990s, and at least 3 percent each year since 2000. Severe droughts in some years reduced these figures. The economy is very dependent on favorable rainfall and other climatic conditions. There are also other problems. A young population means that hundreds of thousands of new jobs are needed every year. Wages are also low. Many who cannot find adequate employment at home go in search of better salaries elsewhere. Last but by no means least, there is a significant "informal sector" of the economy, which escapes taxation and government control and frequently involves illegal activities.

Above: **Harvesting olives. Olives are an important export.**

Opposite: **Markets still play an important role in the Moroccan economy.**

PRIVATIZATION

The buzzword in Morocco is "privatization." In the 1960s, in the early days of independence, there were high hopes for a liberal economic approach,

A vendor in a wool market.

but instead Morocco, like many newly independent countries, found itself attempting to control economic development through central planning. In succeeding years, public utilities, dam and irrigation projects, major chemical industries, the production of tea, sugar, and tobacco, and many other crucial concerns were placed under state control. Similarly, certain economic services such as the marketing of agricultural produce and other products abroad were centrally coordinated to the benefit of the farming industry.

Initially all went fairly well, but after a while the economy lost momentum. Oil prices rose dramatically and drought adversely affected agriculture and the production of hydroelectricity. A continually rising birth rate aggravated unemployment and put a great strain on health and education facilities and on Morocco's ability to feed itself. Conflicts, such as the controversy over Western Sahara, were another drain on the treasury.

Heavily in debt, Morocco applied to the International Monetary Fund, the World Bank, and other international bodies for assistance and set about implementing various policies that, it is hoped, will eventually remedy the situation. Structural reforms, including a gradual reduction in public expenditure and a general process of liberalization and diversification of the economy, got under way in 1986. There have been many setbacks, but progress is slowly being made and essential foreign investment is growing.

Numerous enterprises in agriculture, in the food, banking, and financial sectors, in textiles, leather, and other areas of industrial production, and in tourism and other services have been privatized. State assets in hotels, sugar production, road transportation, petroleum distribution, petrochemicals, housing, textiles, and cement have been sold, and Morocco is now committed to free-market policies with the privatization of all but a few strategic industries, such as phosphate mining, and key public utilities and services.

IMPORTS

Morocco's climate often affects its ability to produce enough food, especially grain and dairy items. For this reason, it has to import substantial quantities of food and drink along with tobacco and sugar. The lack of fuel for energy means that crude oil has to be imported.

Food, drink, tobacco, energy, and lubricants account for about a third of Morocco's expenditure on imports. Capital goods, such as raw materials and machinery, account for around a quarter of the import bill, and semi-finished products absorb a similar amount.

The food bill may decrease as food production increases, but a drop in the fuel bill is unlikely. Morocco has only limited natural energy resources—a little coal, a little oil, and some natural gas. The expansion of hydroelectric output is limited because water supplies are severely affected by periodic droughts. Demand for electricity is expected to double every 10 years, and Morocco is currently importing electric power from the Algerian grid.

Saudi Arabia supplies 25 percent of Morocco's imported oil. The United Arab Emirates supply 19 percent, Iran 13 percent, and Libya and Cameroon 5 percent each.

Farms are small and much of the work is done by hand.

AGRICULTURE

Agriculture plays a pivotal role in the economy despite the fact that farms are small in size, averaging less than 12 acres each. Furthermore, few small farmers have electricity or running water, and communication in outlying areas leaves much to be desired. Another worry is that the average age of farmers is over 50, and between two-thirds and three-quarters are illiterate. Despite these disadvantages, the agricultural sector provides employment for 40 percent of the nearly 10 million workforce.

Farm products are responsible for 17 percent of total exports, and the industry is expanding both in terms of products and new markets. Production of fresh fruit and vegetables is complemented by related industries focusing on animal feed, fruit and vegetable processing, dairy products, and sugar byproducts.

Fertile plains and plateaus, a variety of temperate and semiarid climates, and a long growing season permit the production of a wide range of vegetables and fruit. Although production levels tend to be erratic because of climatic conditions, especially periodic droughts, investment in irrigation programs is slowly bringing the problem under control.

Climate and location ensure that Moroccan fruit and vegetables are ready a few weeks earlier than similar crops in southern Europe, providing a competitive edge.

IRRIGATION PROGRAMS

Morocco has 19.25 million acres of arable land, but only 2 million acres are constantly irrigated. These 2 million acres, however, employ one in three of all agricultural workers in Morocco. They also account for three quarters of all agricultural exports and for 90 percent of their value. These figures amply demonstrate the advantages of irrigation, and steps are currently being taken to develop the full potential of numerous underground water supplies. The problem, however, is that overuse of underground aquifers can rapidly deplete them and cause a collapse of agriculture in areas dependent on them—a possibility that Morocco's fragile economy cannot afford. Today the emphasis is on developing sustainable water sources through the building of dams and canals and through more efficient use of existing irrigation programs, in which a great deal of water is wasted. In 2004 the government of Morocco entered into a public-private partnership irrigation project. The new project will build and manage an irrigation network that will channel water from a dam complex to some 600 citrus farmers in the 10,000-hectare citrus-growing area of Guerdane.

The programs already in place have had remarkable results, particularly in making diversification possible. During the 1990s Morocco successfully opened up markets in Europe for a wide range of its farm produce, including potatoes, squash, melons, strawberries, artichokes, chilis, green beans, and cut flowers. Today some Moroccan produce even reaches the United States.

FISHING

Fishing, along with processing and canning operations, employs more than 400,000 people in Morocco and accounts for a billion dollars of income. The seas along the country's 2,180 miles (3,488 km) of coastline are rich in sardines and anchovies—chances are that some of those in your local supermarket are from Morocco. A wide range of seafood products is now exported from Morocco; this includes lobster, swordfish, tuna, and shellfish.

The busy fishing port of Agadir.

MINERAL RESOURCES

Currently Morocco supplies about one-third of all phosphates used worldwide. It is the largest phosphates exporter in the world and owns three-quarters of the world's phosphate reserves. At present production levels, it is estimated that this represents enough phosphates to meet total demand for 100 years. Deposits of other minerals—iron ore, cobalt, manganese, lead, zinc, copper, fluorite, and anthracite—are useful but pale into insignificance by comparison.

In the 1970s, after the spectacular rise in the price of oil, phosphate prices also rose, and Morocco invested heavily in developing this valuable industry. When the price of oil fell a few years later, the price of phosphates also came down. This collapse, along with the cost of importing oil and the effects of severe drought, forced Morocco into debt. In the long term, however, the investment has proved worthwhile.

A phosphate-related processing plant. The phosphate industry today, together with expanding related industries like the production of phosphoric acid and chemical fertilizers, is a mainstay of the economy.

CASABLANCA—ECONOMIC CAPITAL

Efficient, streamlined Casablanca is Morocco's busiest port and the center of business and banking activities. Well over half the country's industry is located on its outskirts, and the main street boasts impressive skyscrapers.

Despite its modern appearance, the city has a long and turbulent history going back to ancient times. In the 12th century it was a small village known as Anfa. Subsequently it became a refuge for pirates and was twice destroyed by the Portuguese, once in 1468 and again in 1515.

In 1755 the town was destroyed again, this time by the Lisbon earthquake. When the town was rebuilt it was called Dar el Beida, Arabic for "white house." Later, when the Spaniards were authorized to trade in the city, they changed its name to Casa Blanca, Spanish for "white house."

MANUFACTURING

The production of textiles and leather goods is responsible for about 20 percent of exports. About one-third of all industrial workers are employed in spinning, weaving, knitting, and the production of clothing and shoes. Sophisticated textile factories turn out large quantities of ready-made clothing and accessories for world markets.

Morocco has long been known for the quality of its leather goods. However, clothing is the largest earner, followed by knitted goods, carpets, shoes, and various fabrics.

Meanwhile, mechanical and engineering industries are growing steadily in importance. Automobile, truck, and other vehicle parts and accessories are produced, and vehicles are assembled for several international automotive companies. Another sector builds and exports household goods such as refrigerators, gas heaters, and water meters, in addition to pumps and irrigation equipment.

The electronics industry is similarly expanding thanks to the existence of a large pool of skilled workers. Products include electronic equipment, such as computers, semiconductors, transistors, electric cables, radio and television sets, electronic games, telecommunications equipment, and electronic assembly lines for other industries.

A tannery in Fès. The city is renowned for its tanneries and its blue-and-white pottery.

Such prestigious companies as Cartier, Christian Dior, and Ted Lapidus have their designer leather and textile products made in Morocco.

TOURISM

Morocco has become a popular destination for tourists, especially those who come from Europe in search of sunshine and a different culture. Tourism is a flourishing business in Morocco.

The beauty and variety of the landscape is a feast for the senses. Oases spring from the desert, wildflowers bloom in mountain valleys, and snow-clad peaks tower above ancient cities. For beach lovers, sand, sun, and sea are available along the rocky Mediterranean coast and along the Atlantic seaboard, where fine resorts overlook glorious bays and vast stretches of golden sand. There is also much to attract the sports-minded visitor, especially golf and skiing.

Morocco is a treasure house of exotic sights and sounds. The four imperial cities are filled with ancient mosques and palaces. Local dress and customs are colorful, and the bustling markets overflow with handcrafted souvenirs.

An Agadir beach cafe draws tourists in search of sun and scenery.

Given such attractions, it is not surprising that tourism is an important segment of Morocco's economy. The country is generally seen as exciting but safe; however, the Casablanca bombings in 2003 and the association of a few Moroccans with other international terrorist incidents have deterred some people from traveling there. In addition the standards of hygiene, public accommodation, transportation, and amenities are often far below what people in developed countries are comfortable with.

To a large extent these problems are the result of Morocco's isolation from the outside world until fairly recent times. Modern Western standards and aggressive marketing techniques are only slowly being learned. Similarly, the need for adequate standards in terms of good accommodations, facilities, information, and communications has not yet been fully met. On the other hand, isolation has had advantages. More than anywhere else in North Africa, Morocco has retained old traditions and lifestyles; these alone are potent tourist attractions.

MOROCCAN ADVENTURES

The lonely expanses of Morocco's vast interior are the focus of adventure tours. Increasing numbers of visitors seek exciting excursions trekking through remote areas, sometimes accompanied by a mule train and often sleeping in tents. Farther south, camel and Jeep safaris reveal the strange beauty of the desert and the pre-Saharan valleys. Whitewater rafting also caters to those who crave the thrill of speed and danger.

The *souk* (sook), or market, in Marrakech is the center of much economic activity.

THE INFORMAL SECTOR

Morocco has a traditional and flourishing informal sector that provides employment for hundreds of thousands of workers. There are various reasons for its existence. Many businesses conceal their activities because labor laws make it difficult and expensive to fire employees. Some industrialists feel that government inspectors are harsh in their treatment of entrepreneurs; this encourages people to cheat. Low salaries for civil servants also create problems: those who should enforce various duties and taxes often have little incentive to do so.

Another informal but very important part of the Moroccan economy is workers' remittances: money that Moroccans who live in other countries send home to their families. In 2004 this amounted to income of $3.5 billion, either sent in as money orders or carried in as cash.

Unfortunately, many of the activities within this sector of the economy are also outside the law, such as the flourishing production of kif, or hashish, as it is more widely known outside Morocco. This trade is calculated by some to account

A rural Moroccan woman tends to her flock of sheep.

for 70 percent of Europe's annual consumption and is said to be worth around $2 billion a year.

There is also a substantial smuggling industry. Illegal imports through the two Spanish enclaves in the north (Ceuta and Melilla) include alcohol, which retails at about one-third of the average European price in Casablanca, and expensive consumer items such as stereos and computers. Large numbers of cars, perhaps up to 40,000 a year, are stolen in Europe and smuggled into Morocco for sale, while fish caught by Moroccan fishermen are sold on the high seas in exchange for foreign currency.

Many home industries suffer as a result of these illegal activities, and the government loses significant amounts of revenue. Even more serious perhaps are the effects on the future expansion of the Moroccan economy. Foreign investment is essential, but until these problems are addressed, potential investors are hesitant to put their trust in Morocco.

ENVIRONMENT

THE TRADITIONAL MOROCCAN WAY OF LIFE had very little impact on the environment: the combination of a simple livelihood, few material needs, and a habit of not being wasteful resulted in people living in harmony with the environment. This way of life prevailed well into the 19th century in Morocco. It was the introduction of a Western model of capitalism and consumption, brought by Morocco's colonial powers, that began to shift the balance toward people's needs and desires, and away from the needs of the environment.

The 20th century brought many of the environment-related problems to Morocco that are found in other developing countries: a mushrooming population that is forced to rely on natural resources that have been considerably depleted by colonial occupation and exportation. Along with this, Morocco tried to modernize at least fast enough to keep pace with other developing nations, and this often meant that environmental concerns were of secondary importance. Agricultural development had to keep pace with population growth as much as possible so that people had enough to eat, but this often meant developing land for cultivation and the rearing of livestock in ways that were not sustainable and that had long-term negative implications for the environment.

In the 21st century Morocco is not only developing its ability to compete in world markets but also assessing the demands on its environment and natural resources, and for the first time it is taking steps to safeguard what is left for future generations. In 1995, under

Above: **Moroccans have lived harmoniously with their environment for centuries.**

Opposite: **Dades Valley. One of the many spots in Morocco where the environment still remains relatively unspoilt.**

Groundwater being pumped into a storage basin in Tinfou, a town at the edge of the Sahara Desert.

King Hassan II, Morocco formed an environment ministry whose responsibility is to safeguard Morocco's natural resources and fragile ecosystems. The current king has committed Morocco to numerous international environmental treaties and accords.

WATER

If Morocco's main environmental concerns could be summed up in one word, that word would be water. Morocco is largely a desert country, and where rain does fall, it does not do so dependably or predictably. Yet water is needed for every conceivable use: for drinking and washing at home; for agriculture, to produce food for domestic consumption and for export; and for generating electricity at hydroelectric dams. In good years, when rain or winter snowfall fills up reservoirs, the country can make good use of all the water available. When rainfall is below average, however, the economy is severely affected, because prosperity in Morocco largely depends on enough rain falling at the right time. Morocco is now officially a "water-stressed" country, and predictions are that if strong measures are not taken now, it will become water-deficient by 2020.

Many international organizations are helping Morocco plan for the future so that there will be enough water for all of its many uses, but it is not clear at this point that success will be achieved without great sacrifice. The population grows without regard to the water supply, which makes the need ever greater. The economy is geared for growth, and when water supplies run short, economic plans often come to ruin. Underground water supplies, or aquifers, have already been depleted in some areas to a level that is considered dangerous for the future.

Morocco's ever-growing demand for water has resulted in the depletion of water resources in some parts of the country.

Heavy traffic on a street in Marrakech. Air pollution has become an issue of increasing concern among Moroccans living in cities and towns.

SOMETHING IN THE AIR

A major source of air pollution is the exhaust from cars and trucks. While Morocco has a relatively low rate of car ownership compared to Western countries and many people drive smaller motorized vehicles such as mopeds, the auto exhaust problem is still considerable, especially in Morocco's cities. This is due to three factors: emission control standards in Morocco are very low or almost nonexistent; many vehicles in Morocco run on leaded fuel, which is more polluting (although new cars must use unleaded fuel); and many vehicles in Morocco, including private cars, run on diesel fuel, which is more polluting than gasoline. All of this adds up to the fact that Moroccans who live in cities are forced to breathe very low-quality air every day.

THE EARTH VERSUS THE PEOPLE

There are many examples of the conflicts that arise between maintaining a sustainable environment on the one hand and a growing population and economy on the other. Here are a few examples that affect life in Morocco.

Morocco has grown to become one of the largest exporters of olives in the world, second only to Greece. Many areas of Morocco are ideal for growing olives, and Moroccan olives are arguably second to none. Olive oil is another product of the olive industry that brings profits to Morocco. But olives cannot be grown and processed without environmental

Besides stripping the soil of its nutrients, olive trees also use up water, a precious resource in water-scarce Morocco.

Bottled gas and electricity are very expensive, so many Moroccans use firewood. But the trees are dwindling, and Morocco cannot afford to lose any more of its valuable forests.

consequences. Land that is developed for olive groves becomes unsuitable for any other agricultural use: olive trees live for decades and strip the soil of its nutrients. In addition, the factories that process raw olives are sources of environmental pollution.

As Morocco tries to expand its share of the market for fresh produce in Europe, it must find more land to farm. This means clearing forests, overworking the soil in some cases, and using more water, which is already in short supply.

Phosphate revenues contribute significantly to Morocco's economy, but at a considerable cost to the natural environment. The processing of phosphates is chemical-intensive, and the areas of the country where phosphates are mined and produced have very poor environmental conditions. Not only is there phosphate dust in the air constantly but even the local water supplies have an unpleasant taste and people are forced to rely on expensive mineral water.

Morocco's long coastline is home to some of the finest beaches on either the Atlantic or the Mediterranean. However, many of Morocco's most populous urban areas are also on these two coasts, and they are growing phenomenally as people abandon rural areas and seek their fortunes in the city. Infrastructure cannot keep pace with the growth, and this means that raw sewage is often pumped into the sea near cities. Most tourists already avoid the beaches that are directly adjacent to Rabat and Casablanca because of fear of disease, although Moroccans still use them.

RECYCLING

Morocco has almost no modern recycling facilities but, so far, it has little need for them. There are several reasons for this, and they can be summarized under the old adage "waste not, want not."

The items that North Americans recycle most—glass bottles, plastic containers, metal cans, and paper—exist in Morocco but are not treated the same way. Not very many foods are sold in glass jars, and people find different uses at home for the few glass jars that they might accumulate. Soft drinks are sold in glass bottles that go back to the bottling plant to be refilled. Although food vendors do not often reuse plastic containers and metal cans, their customers often find other uses for the empty containers.

The most common packaging for food is reused paper. Vendors in markets often wrap the purchase in newspaper, and if you buy spices or snacks on the street in small amounts, chances are it will be wrapped in notebook paper with a student's writing on it!

When Moroccans go to the markets, they always carry a reusable shopping bag and fill it up with their purchases as they go from stall to stall. Plastic bags are available from the vendors, and these have caused one of Morocco's worst pollution problems: many beautiful countryside landscapes are spoiled by the presence of ripped and shredded plastic bags clinging to shrubs and trees.

Rural areas in Morocco have no trash collection facilities and generally do not need them. Everything left over is put to some other use; goats and other domestic animals eat vegetable peelings and table scraps.

MOROCCANS

IN DAYS GONE BY, the inhabitants of North Africa, especially large parts of modern Algeria and Morocco, were known to the Europeans as Moors. As groups of Arabs moved into the area from the east and began to mingle with the indigenous Berber people, the word "Moor" was used to describe people of mixed Berber and Arab ancestry. The name came from the Greek word *mauros* but was probably of North African origin. In more recent times the French called the country *le Maroc* and its people *les marrocains*—which evolved into today's "Morocco" and "Moroccans."

In the Middle Ages, Moors were commonly thought to be Negroid in appearance. By the 16th century, enough was known about the people of North Africa and their increasing intermingling with various peoples from sub-Saharan Africa for Shakespeare to present his Prince of Morocco in *The Merchant of Venice* as "tawny," while two other Shakespearean Moors are black. A variety of peoples make up today's Moroccans, including Berbers, Arabs, and sub-Saharan Africans. Most Moroccans are of mixed ancestry.

The Moorish character has been misunderstood due to ignorance of the culture. History reveals the Moroccans to be a people of rugged determination and courage, tolerant of other Islamic sects and other religions. Meanwhile, Moroccans' generous hospitality and regard for family values are almost legendary.

Below and Opposite: **There is a variety of appearances in modern Moroccans, from Sub-Saharan Africans to light-skinned Berbers and Arabs.**

57

POPULATION FACTS AND FIGURES

The vast majority of Moroccans are Berber, Arab, or a mixture of the two. There is also a significant sub-Saharan African presence in the population, as a result of centuries of contact with the rest of Africa. Morocco is almost 100 percent Muslim, but there is a small and visible Jewish minority that lives mostly in the cities of Rabat, Casablanca, and Oujda. Foreigners in Morocco, numbering about 60,000, are mainly European, but there are also a significant number of Arabs from Middle Eastern countries.

The population is concentrated in the western part of Morocco on the fertile plains and in the coastal areas. Most industrial and economic activity is also located here. So too are all the large cities, except for Oujda in the northeast.

The official census of 2004, which included residents of Western Sahara, revealed a total population of just under 30 million (29,891,708, to be exact). Also, for the first time, Morocco was found to have a larger urban than rural population.

The Moroccan population is overwhelmingly young.

It has succeeded in reducing its growth rate only marginally; it is still overwhelmingly a young country, with nearly half of the population under 20 years of age and about 70 percent younger than 25.

The large number of young people puts a great strain on the economy. Morocco desperately needs skilled workers and executives, so about one-quarter of the national budget is spent on education, but there are still not enough facilities for everyone. About half of all the men

(and even more of the women) can neither read nor write, and this traps great numbers of workers in low-paid, unskilled jobs.

Some people regard family planning as an essential part of the answer to the problem, but in the 1960s, suggestions that family size could be controlled were rejected by the government and by conservative Moroccans on the grounds that contraception runs counter to Islamic culture. In recent years, however, the king himself has spoken publicly about the need for family planning. Ideas that at one time would have been considered anti-religious are being aired discreetly and slowly accepted.

MOROCCANS ABROAD

More than 5 million Moroccans live and work abroad because of the lack of employment and low wages at home. There are 840,000 Moroccans in France, 273,000 in the Netherlands, and 203,000 in Belgium, while Italy, Spain, and Germany together play host to approximately 600,000.

In Africa, Libya and Algeria have a total Moroccan population of 220,000, and smaller numbers are scattered in various Muslim countries around the world.

Large parts of Morocco are sparsely populated. Ninety percent of the population lives north of a diagonal line drawn between the plain surrounding the Sous River near Agadir in the southwest and Oujda in the northeast.

59

Berber women frequently tattoo their faces.

BERBERS—THE INDIGENOUS PEOPLE

The indigenous people of Morocco are the Berbers, who are known to have lived since the beginning of recorded history in largely scattered tribes in the areas of North Africa that are now Morocco, Algeria, Tunisia, Libya, and Egypt. Little is known for certain about Berber origins, but the high cheekbones, fair coloring, and occasional green or blue eyes found among them suggest that they have European connections or that they are Euro-Asiatics. In any case, they were never a single, homogeneous group, but a collection of tribes living in different areas, with different lifestyles and languages, and with diverse physical and cultural characteristics.

The Berbers have lived alongside people of Arab origin for around 1,200 years. They intermarried with them and were converted to Islam. A very large number also adopted Arabic as their language. Even so, the Berbers claim that they have never been conquered. It is perhaps more accurate to say that the Phoenicians and the Carthaginians had little

BERBERS FROM BARBARY!

The Arabs were probably responsible for coining the word "Berber" to describe the indigenous peoples of North Africa. It is likely they adopted the word from the Greek *bárbaros*, which was used to mean "those who are foreign," that is, not Greek. Among the Arabs, Berber indicated people who were not of Arab origin, and for many centuries Barbary was the name given to Berber-occupied parts of North Africa. *Bárbaros* is also the root of "barbarian" and "barbaric" because the "highly civilized" Greeks felt that people who did not speak their language were at best uncivilized and at worst savage.

interest in conquering them and that the Romans had only limited success in subduing a few tribes in the interior. In the seventh century, when small numbers of Arabs began to arrive, the Berbers were impressed by the Arabs' desire for expansion and their missionary zeal. Little by little the various indigenous tribes were converted to Islam, but even within this common religious framework the Berbers retained their power for about 500 years.

A succession of Muslim Berbers ruled a number of independent kingdoms. They included camel-riding desert nomads, quiet farming people from the High and Anti-Atlas, and tribes that edged in slowly from the empty area between present-day Taza and Algeria in search of better pasture for their flocks. Thereafter, newly arriving Arab groups gained the upper hand and displaced the Berbers as the dominant power in Morocco.

It is difficult to say what proportion of the total population is Berber. Perhaps 60 percent have Berber blood, but only about one-third habitually speak a Berber language rather than Arabic, which is the national language. Berbers today are moving to the cities; they also form the bulk of the Moroccans forced by unemployment to seek work outside the country.

By and large today's Moroccan Berbers live in the mountainous countryside, but in recent years many have moved into urban areas.

The traditional *fez* is rarely worn today.

ARABS FROM THE EAST

The name "Arab" is loosely given to people whose native language is Arabic. By and large, Moroccan Arabs are descendants of Arabs who intermarried with the indigenous Berbers.

The first Arabs arrived in Morocco in the late seventh century. After the death of the Prophet Mohammed in 632, his followers embarked on careers of conquest in search of land and riches, and filled with missionary zeal, they sought to carry the message of their new religion far and wide. After conquests to the east of Arabia, they turned westward to the lands stretching along the northern coast of Africa.

In 683 Arab commander Oqba ben Nafi led his army into what is now Morocco and spurred his horse into the Atlantic Ocean, shouting triumphantly that only the sea prevented him from carrying his conquest any farther. He called the African territory he conquered *el Maghreb*, meaning "the West." Morocco he called *el Maghreb el-Aqsa*, or "the farthest West." Today Morocco, Algeria, and Tunisia are still known as the Maghreb countries.

By 711 most of North Africa had come under Islamic control, although only about 100,000 Arabs had been involved in the conquest of this vast tract of the continent. In the next five centuries waves of relatively small

Originally the name "Arab" applied only to people living in the Arabian Peninsula, but today it describes around 100 million people living in the Middle East and North Africa and large minorities in other parts of the world.

groups of Arabs reached Morocco and settled there. Some were dissidents who moved westward to escape the fighting over who should succeed Mohammed as the leader of Islam; others were refugees fleeing violent disputes over the interpretation of the Koran—the Islamic holy book.

The style of conquest varied. One group created Fès, the first of the four imperial cities, and established Arab authority in the north of the country, but another group was likened to "an army of locusts destroying everything in their path." Various communities settled peacefully along the northern edge of the Sahara Desert or in the southern coastal plains. Mostly they played no major role in Moroccan life until the middle of the 16th century, when turbulence among the Berbers brought them to power.

Arabs were never numerous, but the Berbers adopted their religion, and many adopted their language. Life in the large cities where the Arabs congregated was greatly influenced by Arab and Islamic culture, and Berbers in many parts of the countryside found their sedentary way of life undermined by the arrival of more dynamic, nomadic tribes. Only the mountain areas escaped this disruption to traditional lifestyles.

It is difficult to distinguish Arabs from Berbers.

AN ARAB NATION?

Moroccans are regarded as Arabs in an Arab country for two reasons: the monarch claims direct descent from the Prophet Mohammed, and most of the people speak Arabic. Although Morocco is not ethnically an Arab nation, Moroccans identify, emotionally, with the Arab world.

Moroccans have long been a people of mixed race. In their veins runs the blood of many races—indigenous Berbers, Arabs who settled in Morocco over a period of around six centuries, slaves imported from sub-Saharan Africa, and immigrants from Spain who were themselves a mixture of Arab, Berber, and native Iberian. Physical appearance is not a reliable guide. It is virtually impossible, and with a few exceptions, meaningless, to distinguish Arab from Berber. Today the people of Morocco regard themselves primarily as Moroccans.

THE REAL DIVIDE

An Arab-Berber divide does exist, but it is geographic rather than ethnic. Broadly speaking, there are two groups of Moroccans—those who live in urban areas and those who live in the countryside. The Arabic-speaking majority is concentrated in the lowlands and in the cities, although there are isolated groups of mainly Arab people in areas that are otherwise predominantly Berber. Those who speak mainly Berber, on the other hand, generally inhabit the poorer mountain areas. They account for between 35 and 40 percent of the population. However, little by little, Berbers are leaving the countryside and drifting into the towns in search of better-paid work and better educational and health facilities.

In the 1930s, when the French attempted to set Arabs against Berbers in order to facilitate French control, the plan misfired. This attempt at manipulation by a common enemy brought the two together, and Arabs openly prayed, "Oh God, separate us not from our Berber brothers."

LIFESTYLE

EVERY MOROCCAN drinks mint tea. It is the national drink—an amber-colored, fragrant liquid, served piping hot in small glasses, and heavily sweetened with sugar. It is refreshing and thirst-quenching even when the weather is stiflingly hot. At other times, on cool or damp days, a glass of hot tea is a warming and revitalizing refreshment.

Mint tea is jokingly nicknamed "Moroccan whiskey," but it plays a more essential role in Moroccan life than whiskey in its native Scotland. Few business deals are concluded without several glasses of tea, and the making and serving of tea is a focal point of Moroccan hospitality. Its preparation is both serious and leisurely and emphasizes the importance placed on hospitality as a part of daily life. A guest invited to make the tea is conscious of being made very welcome and highly honored.

The tea-making ritual is elaborate and dignified. The necessary implements are a round-bellied teapot with a conical lid, small glasses, and three boxes containing respectively green tea, chunks of white sugar, and sprigs of mint. The tea is put in the pot, and boiling water is added along with large quantities of sugar and handfuls of mint.

The liquid is left to infuse for a while, then a little is poured out for sampling—an action often carried out with all the concentration of a connoisseur tasting wine. More sugar or mint is added if required. Finally, it is ready. The tea maker raises the pot with a flourish, holds it high above the glasses, and fills each one to the brim.

Opposite: **Rural Moroccans draw water from a common well.**

Below: **Tea was introduced into Morocco by British merchants in 1854, when the Crimean War forced them to look for new markets. Moroccans adopted the new drink with great enthusiasm but adapted it to suit their sweet tooth and flavored it with fresh mint.**

A DIFFERENT SENSE OF TIME

The Moroccan delight in offering hospitality implies a certain attitude toward time. The making of tea takes time, a celebratory meal takes time to prepare and time to eat, and conversing courteously with guests or with business colleagues is not something to be hurried. Buying and selling also require a generous investment of time.

In general, Moroccans have not yet been affected by the frenetic pace of modern life typical of cities in the West. They proceed on the assumption that when God made time, he made plenty of it! The completion of a business deal, adequate rainfall, or the solutions to one's problems—all these things will come in the goodness of time and, most importantly, provided God is willing. The phrase *Insha'Allah* (in-SHAH-lah), which translates as "If God wills" or "God willing," is heard over and over again in conversations and even in public announcements.

This does not mean that life in Morocco is totally relaxed. On the contrary, although doing business is considerably more time-consuming than in most developed countries, the Moroccan businessperson is efficient, and, when necessary, business can be fast and furious.

Abortion facilities are not officially available in Morocco, but more Moroccan women than before are using birth control. Few Moroccan couples today want a large family, in contrast to previous generations who believed that having a large family was their duty.

TRANSPORTATION

Mile upon mile of dirt tracks and rough trails wind across lonely mountain and desert terrain, but there is also a network of good roads that serve the urban and western parts of the country and link them with more remote and distant centers of population. Freeways are still rare—there are three—one connecting Casablanca and Rabat, another between Fés and Marrakech, and one that connects Rabat and Tangier—but more are planned and some are under construction.

Morocco possesses excellent transportation systems—probably the best in North Africa. An efficient rail network complements the road network and connects the main towns of the north and the coast, as well as Marrakech, while the international airport at Casablanca links Morocco to the outside world.

Public transportation is good and not outrageously expensive for the average Moroccan. The very poorest have to make do with their donkeys and mules; the slightly better off use one of the various bus systems or "*grand taxis.*" "*Grands,*" or collective taxis, are usually big Peugeot or Mercedes models that run on regular routes. Three or four passengers crowd into the back, and another one or two share the front seat with the driver.

In the cities, the most common form of transportation after the public bus is the ubiquitous little taxi. It is easily recognizable by its color (yellow in Marrakech, for instance) and its roof racks with the decoratively inscribed words "*Petit Taxi.*" In the countryside the roads demand more robust vehicles such as trucks, pickups, and Land Rovers—in short, any form of transportation that can survive the bone-shaking experience of dirt and rock-strewn roads.

The Moroccan who is wealthy enough to own motorized transportation is most likely to have a moped of some kind. These are said to outnumber cars by 500 to one.

A busy street in Casablanca.

CITY LIFE

The maze of narrow, winding streets is a distinctive feature of the Moroccan *medina*.

Morocco only recently became a country with a larger urban than rural population; the latest census showed that 57 percent of Moroccans now live in towns and cities. Cities in Morocco present a fascinating contrast of the old and the new.

Today virtually every large town or city with any degree of history has three distinct parts—the *medina*, the modern town, and the *souk*. *Medinas* are Arab-built, often medieval areas, usually a labyrinthine maze of narrow, winding streets and passages filled with small workshops and humble homes. At worst they are slums populated by the poor. At best they are ancient walled cities humming with vitality, though often lacking in basic amenities.

In the *medinas*, light filters in through trellises above crowded lanes. Here carts laden with goods jostle for room with children carrying trays of dough to the bakeries, brightly dressed women, some veiled some not, and men in *djellabas*. The air is filled with sounds: the pleas of beggars, vendors shouting their wares, hawking and spitting, and the clatter of hammers in the metal workshops. Amid the din the gentle clip-clop of hooves on cobbles can hardly be heard, but harsh cries of "*Balak!*" (BAA-lek) or "Look out!" alert passersby to the danger of being pushed against the wall by an overloaded donkey or run down by a tradesperson in a hurry.

Separate quarters are devoted to the making and selling of different items: embroidered slippers, jewelry,

70

teapots and trays, carved wooden furniture, and carpets and rugs. The entrances to homes and workshops are often little more than holes in the wall. The same may be true of an exquisite mosque or a grand palace—treasure houses of fine stucco and woodcarving, somber mosaics, and shady, serene patios with fountains and flowers.

Medinas also include *souks*, or market areas where Moroccans shop for meat, fruit, vegetables, and other foodstuffs, as well as for household goods, spices, perfumes, cosmetics, aphrodisiacs, magic potions, and fresh mint to flavor their tea.

FRENCH-STYLE MODERN TOWNS

It was fortunate for Morocco that the first resident-general of the French Protectorate was an enlightened military officer sympathetic toward the culture of the people he was sent to "protect." The country desperately needed modern sites for government and administration, but rather than pull down or adapt existing structures, Lyautey organized the building of new towns outside the *medinas*.

Many of Morocco's rich—few though they are—have moved to these quiet suburbs and have set up home in whitewashed, flower-smothered, Mediterranean-style modern houses, and blocks of apartments with neat, well-kept gardens.

The "new towns," as they are still called, have grand boulevards that often radiate from a central square, leafy suburbs lined with orange and jacaranda trees, and elegant cafés.

71

RURAL LIFE

Outside the big cities, people congregate in small, dusty towns. In Berber country, homes or even whole villages are *kasbahs*—fortified buildings constructed from *pisé* (PEE-say), a mixture of palm-tree fibers and compressed mud-clay from riverbanks. Elsewhere there are villages carved into or clinging onto the rocky mountainsides, virtually indistinguishable from the natural landscape. Villages in the north are often clusters of whitewashed houses with tiled staircases and small windows with wrought-iron grilles. The desert fringes and remote mountain valleys are dotted with the black tents of nomadic tribes.

WEALTH AND WORK

As in so many developing countries, Morocco has a few rich and many poor, with a slowly emerging middle class. In general there is a big difference between town and country incomes, and living conditions and amenities in country areas are usually worse than those in urban areas. It is significant that the most remote villages are occupied primarily by women, children, and the elderly, because the able-bodied men have migrated to the towns in search of work or higher wages. In addition, every town has its sad quota of beggars—the blind or the maimed, and emaciated women with hands outstretched for a few dirhams to feed their children.

For many people, regardless of where they work, conditions are hard despite the fact that local labor laws are based on International Labor Organization recommendations. Working hours for both sexes are capped at a maximum of a certain number of hours per day or week; all workers must have weekly rest periods of at least 24 consecutive hours and are entitled to paid holidays according to their length of service. It is unfortunate that those in the informal sector can fall through the safety net that these regulations are intended to provide. Another problem is that the physical working conditions can often be appalling, especially in the *medinas*, where numerous health risks make for a short, hard life.

WAGES, SALARIES, AND PRICES

For those lucky enough to have a job, the pay is low. In 2003, for example, the official guaranteed minimum wage was just under 9 dirhams per hour; that translates to less than a dollar per hour. Agricultural workers may sometimes earn no more than 45 dirhams (just under $4) for a whole day's work. The low rate of pay tends to encourage corruption, moonlighting, and tax evasion.

On the other hand, the government of Morocco spends millions of dirhams on subsidies—special expenditures to guarantee the low price of staple foods. Moroccans enjoy relatively affordable sugar, flour, and cooking oil because the government keeps the prices of such commodities low. Without subsidies, many more Moroccans would fall below the poverty line and social unrest would probably follow.

Opposite: **Berber families washing potatoes in the Setti Fatma Valley.**

An estimated 20 percent of the workforce is unemployed or underemployed. Both situations cause poverty and foment discontent. For lack of other employment, well-educated students, for instance, are forced to work as unofficial tour guides, and the search for work drives many Moroccans overseas. Social security provisions to alleviate these problems include temporary food and job programs, but extend only to a small percentage of the workforce.

HEALTH

Ten years ago the average Moroccan who survived infancy could expect to live 62 years. Today the figure has climbed to 68 years, but it is still somewhat low compared to other countries with similar per capita incomes. In terms of stability, religious tolerance, and certain areas of economic progress, Morocco is often compared favorably with its neighbors, but its health record is not as good. In Tunisia, for instance, life expectancy is about the same—68 years—but the infant mortality rate is only 43 per 1,000 births. In Morocco the figure is 62 per 1,000 births—an improvement on the 1985 figure of 85, but still not impressive.

Health facilities are patchy. People in rural areas and the urban poor are badly served and in particular need access to clean, safe water. Malnutrition is also common in both these groups. Medical services and personnel tend to be concentrated in urban areas, with the exception of the remote Western Sahara. Here, in what most people would consider the back of beyond, hospitals and health centers have been built and equipped to high standards, and medicine and operations are free. This is all part of a policy to reinforce Morocco's claim to the territory by attracting Moroccans to the area and making it desirable to stay.

In 2003 only 53 adults in every 100 could read. The figure for women is lower.

EDUCATION

The emphasis on education is relatively recent and is beset with many problems: cost, lack of teachers, lack of buildings, remote communities, and a rapidly expanding population. Education is compulsory for Moroccans between the ages of 7 and 15 and includes five years of primary school followed by three or four years in a secondary or a technical school.

By no means do all Moroccan children go to school. As in the case of health facilities, and for the same reason, people in Western Sahara fare better than their compatriots elsewhere. In El Aaiún, the provincial capital, 90 percent of school-age children attend school. In other parts of Morocco, especially in small, isolated communities or where family poverty means children have to work alongside their parents, the figure is much lower. Priority is still often given to educating boys.

Despite so many problems, however, increasing numbers of students pass through the education system and enroll in institutes of higher education and local universities to study medicine, law, business, the liberal arts, the sciences, and mining. A lucky few receive financial assistance to study overseas, usually in France. However, talented students returning home eager for employment and the opportunity to put into practice new ideas learned overseas are often frustrated when trying to reach their goals.

A large proportion of the older generations cannot read or write. Illiteracy in the rural areas is worse than in the towns, and everywhere the figures are worse for women.

Students outside the University of Fès. In February 1994 there were violent clashes between radical Islamic and left-wing students at Fès University. Dozens of students were arrested, and courses at the university were suspended indefinitely.

Family life is of great
importance to Moroccans.

THE CORNERSTONE OF SOCIETY

Family life is regarded as the cornerstone of Morrocan society, and great emphasis is placed on family values, family cohesion, and hospitality. A wedding, the birth of a child, and the circumcision of a young boy are all cause for much rejoicing, celebration, and ritual.

There was a time when all marriages were arranged, with eligible young men and women obediently marrying according to their parents' choices. Quite possibly neither party had much contact with the other before the first stage in the marriage negotiations—the formal agreement that was signed a year or two before the ceremony.

Today educated Moroccans increasingly prefer and are able to choose their own partners, and many opt for a simpler ceremony rather than the elaborate 15-day event of the past, with its strict protocol and high expense. Also disappearing to a large extent is the presence of a third party on the wedding night to verify the bride's virginity and the consummation of the marriage.

Moroccan law permits polygamy. In accordance with Islamic practice, a Moroccan man may take up to four wives, but he is required to provide for all of them equally. Very few Moroccan women today are willing to accept the presence of a second wife in their home.

Another factor discouraging polygamy is cost. A wedding is an expensive affair made even more costly by the traditional gifts presented to the bride's family. The rising cost of marriage, along with recession and reduced employment possibilities, means that many young people are having to marry later than they formerly did.

HOUSE AND HOME

"Privacy" is the key word in Moroccan family life. Homes are inward-looking. Rooms typically open onto a central courtyard, and the largely blank exterior walls hide patios and gardens decorated as finance and taste permit. Even modern houses in the French-built new towns retain this private aspect.

In the *medinas* it is possible to move from one house to another across the flat roofs, and there was a time when this was the extent of a woman's freedom to move around. In many villages, the houses are still built to fit the space available, one against the other, with interior patios visible to the outsider only from above.

Looking into the interior courtyard of a Moroccan house.

77

WOMEN

It is common to see female students confidently striding out in short skirts and heels, their hair cut in Western styles, with not a veil or scarf in sight.

Muslim women are often regarded by the non-Muslim world as uniformly downtrodden individuals, little more than useful chattel in a men's world. In Morocco this is not the case. Moroccan women are subject to the same constraints as women in other Muslim countries—they keep a low profile in public and their place is definitely in the home—but in the big cities at least, customs have changed considerably. Today women ride scooters, drive cars, and occasionally eat and even discreetly smoke in public.

One notable development in recent years has been the increased resources allocated to education for girls. In 1993 only 46 percent of high-school age girls were enrolled in school, but today two-thirds of them are studying. Most public schools in Morocco are for both sexes, but cities have a few same-sex public schools.

WOMEN'S DRESS

Although more and more women are now going out to work, many still wear a *kaftan*—a long outer garment—and a veil or at least a scarf covering their hair. Older women continue to wear the veil, perhaps more out of tradition than for any other reason, and are often seen with their jeans-clad or short-skirted daughters. Another reason for wearing traditional dress is that it protects

A women's literacy class. Women lag behind men in education.

the fashionable finery underneath. This is often the case with young and obviously emancipated women, where the slit in the side of the *kaftan* reveals clothes that would not be out of place in Europe.

In conservative countryside areas, there are a few predominantly Arab villages where the women continue to be totally enveloped in black. But Berber custom is quite different. Berber women work in the fields, and

although they might modestly draw a headscarf across their faces, veils and *kaftans* are not, as a rule, part of their normal dress. Attire varies from region to region but is unfailingly colorful and consists of long skirts, blouses, and shawls with floral patterns, stripes, or embroidery. Hands are sometimes tinted with henna and faces tattooed.

The *kaftan* is the most common dress for Moroccan women.

TRADITIONAL DRESS

The Moroccan version of the veil, in most cases, is a light and filmy covering for the nose, mouth, and chin. Some veils match the *djellaba* with which they are worn. Others are in contrasting colors. *Kaftans* and women's *djellabas* come in every color of the rainbow. The best are pretty, fashionable garments with expert tailoring, and groups of women can look like clusters of jewel-colored butterflies.

Men also wear *djellabas*. Theirs are normally made of heavier or coarser material, and are not at all colorful. Most are shades of gray, brown, cream, white, or black; a few may be striped. Many men wear the *djellaba* as a matter of course, but others have adopted Western dress.

RELIGION

TOWARD THE END of the seventh century A.D. Arab military missionaries, fired with a fierce desire to convert the world to Islam—the new religion founded by the Prophet Mohammed—turned their attention to the North African coastal plain. Oqba ben Nafi, one of the first Arabs to venture into the wilds of Africa, led his cavalry into what is now modern Morocco around 683.

Despite his successful invasion, Oqba made little attempt to establish long-term control over Morocco. The greater part of the country still remained unconquered, but many northern Berber tribes, attracted by the energy of the new religion and its adherents, willingly converted to Islam.

In subsequent decades, more Arabs arrived, similarly bent both on conquest and on spreading Islam. Their efforts met with varying degrees of success, but it was not until the arrival of Moulay Idriss in 788 that Islam was established as the religion of the majority and a measure of unity was achieved.

Moulay Idriss was welcomed in the ancient Roman city of Volubilis by converted Berber tribesmen. With their aid he set about converting the rest. He proved so successful in this endeavor, and his power in North Africa increased so dramatically, that in 791, rivals as far away as Baghdad sent assassins to poison him.

After his death, he was buried in a small town that he had founded and that bore his name. Today Moulay Idriss is the holiest town in Morocco, and until recently, non-Muslims were not permitted to remain in the town overnight.

Above: **Moulay Idriss (with the green roof) is a shrine in memory of the establishment of Islam in Morocco and a memorial to Moulay Idriss, who played a large role in this enterprise.**

Opposite: **A religious school, or** *medersa*, **in Marrakesh.**

ISLAM IN PRACTICE

The word "Islam" means "submission to God." The belief that lies at the very heart of this religion is that there is only one God—Allah—and that

Mohammed is his prophet. Muslims also believe that the angel Gabriel appeared to Mohammed and dictated the Koran (Islam's holy book) to him. Muslims believe that the Koran contains the word of God detailing how true believers should conduct their lives. The principles expressed in the Koran can be applied to almost every moment of a Muslim's existence. Islam, therefore, is not simply a religion but also a way of life.

Believing and testifying that there is no god but Allah, and that Mohammed is his prophet, is the first of the Five Pillars, or major observances, of Islam. The other four requirements are to pray five times a day, to observe the fast of Ramadan, to give at least a small proportion of one's income to help support the poor and to provide for the upkeep of mosques, and to make a pilgrimage to Mecca, the birthplace of Islam.

To remind believers of their obligations, *muezzins* chanting from the tops of minarets call people to prayer, much as bells are rung in Christian churches to signal that a service is beginning. Muslims can pray wherever they wish, although a mosque is preferable, especially on Friday, which is the Islamic holy day. Friday prayers in the mosque are usually accompanied by a sermon.

Reading the Koran is an important part of Islamic practice.

Ramadan is the ninth month of the Islamic year, and for the duration of the month Muslims do not eat or drink between sunrise and sunset. In Morocco the fast is particularly difficult to observe when Ramadan falls at the height of the summer heat. Sunset, however, brings relief for all Muslims wherever they are, and the evenings are filled with feasting and rejoicing. A final meal is taken just before sunrise, and the fast begins again early in the morning as soon as there is enough light to distinguish between a black thread and a white one.

The pilgrimage to Mecca is required only if there is enough money available for the long journey and the expenses of the pilgrimage.

Giving alms at Fès Mosque. Setting aside a part of one's income for the relief of the poor and the upkeep of mosques is one of the requirements for Muslims.

BREAKING THE RAMADAN FAST

As darkness falls during Ramadan, Moroccans traditionally break their fast with a bowl of *harira* (hah-REER-rah) soup. The basis of this soup is lamb broth enriched with diced lamb, lentils, chickpeas, onions, garlic, fresh herbs, and spices. It is frequently colored with tomatoes and thickened at the last moment with yeast, flour, or beaten eggs.

The soup is often served along with tidbits such as fresh dates, dried figs, hardboiled eggs, and fried, honeyed pastries called *shebbakia* (sherh-BAK-ee-ah).

Boys in a Koran school.

ISLAM IN MOROCCO

For some non-Muslims, Islam is synonymous with intolerance and violent fundamentalism. The average Moroccan, however, although devout and conscientious about his religious duties, is in no way a fanatic.

Geographically Morocco is far removed from the center of Islam and has remained virtually untouched by the often violent conflicts between rival Islamic sects, particularly between the Sunni and Shia sects. The development of Moroccan Islam has also been influenced by Berber religious practices that predate the arrival of the Arabs and their new religion. Finally, in more recent times, Morocco's desire to have good relationships with the West, and particularly with Europe, has brought home the value of avoiding the excesses of extremist fundamentalism, as well as what outsiders might regard as brutal practices.

Morocco has adopted the Western calendar and many Western customs, such as the New Year's Day holiday. Offices and shops close on Sundays rather than on Fridays. That said, even the busiest streets in the biggest towns suddenly become quiet on Friday at midday, and

In May 2003, terrorist bomb attacks in Casablanca killed 41 people. This was a grim awakening for Moroccans, who suddenly realized that their country was not immune to the excesses of Islamic fundamentalism.

84

large congregations flock to the mosques to pray and listen to the Friday sermon. In some rural areas, where few are concerned with business in the Western and urban sense, Friday is still the day of rest, and *souks* are likely to close in the afternoon.

SAINTS AND SHRINES

The Moroccan countryside is dotted with whitewashed, domed buildings called *koubbas* (KOO-bah). These are the tombs of *marabouts* (MAH-rah-boo)—saintly men with a local cult following. In theory, Islam does not accept the idea of there being any intermediary between the individual and God. When Muslims pray, they speak directly to Allah, but Islam in Morocco is tolerant of these cults of saints and their shrines.

Koubbas are especially popular with women, who may visit the tomb of a favorite saint or even a supposedly sacred tree or stream. Generally they ask for favors such as relief from an illness, or plead for intercession. Sometimes a visit is an opportunity to give vent to grief for some misfortune.

Magic and superstitious beliefs are taboo for the strictly orthodox Muslim. But old folk practices die hard, and every *medina* has its fortune-teller as well as shops selling magic potions and strange concoctions that shopkeepers claim protect against evils of one kind or another.

A tomb of a *marabout*. The cult of *marabouts* probably has its roots in early Berber worship focused around individual holy men.

THE MOSQUE

The focus of Muslim religious activity is the mosque, which in many cases has an attached *medersa* (may-DER-sah), or student college. The most obvious sign of the presence of a mosque is the square. Overlooking the square are green minarets from which the *muezzin* calls the faithful to prayer. These days, the *muezzin*'s voice is generally amplified by a loudspeaker, but his words and their message are the same.

The mosque is the meeting place for prayer and usually comprises a courtyard with a fountain and a hall for prayer with aisles separating men from women. A niche in one of the walls indicates the direction of Mecca. This is called the *mihrab* (MEEH-rab) and to its right there is a pulpit called a *minbar*, from which the *imam* (ee-MAM) reads the Koran, preaches his sermons, and leads the congregation in prayer.

"Mosque" is a word meaning "the place where one bows down in prayer." Prayer within the mosque, indeed prayer anywhere, whether in a prayer hall, at home, or elsewhere, involves a fixed number of genuflections and prostrations. This ritual prostration, however, is not usually visible to the tourist in Morocco because non-Muslims are not permitted to enter the mosques (the exception being the Hassan II Mosque).

Muslims demonstrate their respect for the mosque by removing their shoes before entering its precincts. A pile of shoes beside an inconspicuous doorway is often the sign of a mosque entrance and a quick peep through the archway into the courtyard frequently reveals worshippers performing ritual ablutions— washing their hands, face, and feet, often at a central fountain.

MEDERSAS *AND MINARETS*

Medersas are colleges and residence halls that were once attached to the mosques and served as early universities. They also have minarets. Unlike the mosques, Morocco's fine *medersas* are open to all, even though a few may have prayer halls that are still in use and are off limits to non-Muslims.

Some of these residential colleges were built by pious sultans, but many developed from domestic buildings, sometimes the houses of the principal teachers. Either way they alleviated the lot of poor (male) students from the countryside who often had to walk long distances to places of learning. The buildings themselves were elaborately ornamented, but the students generally lived in cell-like rooms, often dark and damp and badly ventilated. Lodging, drinking water, and bread, however, were free. Similar buildings called *zaouias* (za-OO-ee-ahs) were attached to many *koubbas*.

The minaret of El Mansour mosque in Marrakech.

87

THE HASSAN II MOSQUE

Keyhole arches around the esplanade in the Hassan II Mosque.

The inhabitants of Casablanca had long felt that the city lacked an architectural monument, a focus that would put it on an equal footing with the four imperial cities and complement its economic importance. This was remedied in 1993 when the Hassan II Mosque opened for worship providing Morocco's commercial center with a magnificent spiritual heart.

The new mosque is the largest mosque in Africa and is second in size only to the Great Mosque in Mecca. It cost around $750 million, which came partly from government spending, but mostly from contributions from Moroccans all over the country and also abroad. While support was supposed to be voluntary, many Moroccans say that the pressure placed on them to make a contribution was considerable.

Casablanca's new landmark is more than a mosque. The complex also houses a *medersa*, a library, a museum, conference facilities, and even public baths for men and for women. It was built to withstand earthquakes and has laser beams on the minaret that point toward Mecca. Its opening marked the 60th birthday of King Hassan II.

The exterior is decorated in a restful green and white—the Islamic colors for tolerance and peace. A series of sculpted marble columns and characteristic Moroccan keyhole arches enclose the central building, which stands on a vast esplanade that can accommodate 80,000 worshipers. Mosaic decorations, traditional in both color and design, cover fountains and facades, and monumental metal doors glitter in the sunshine. The prayer hall within has room for 20,000 male worshipers. They prostrate themselves on an inlaid marble floor with colors and patterns made to resemble a Moroccan carpet. Women occupy two separate mezzanines and are shielded from view by delicately carved cedarwood screens.

Light filters in through rose windows and large bay windows that look out over the Atlantic Ocean. On fine days the roof over the central court can be opened to the blue sky above. When it is closed, glittering Venetian chandeliers and hundreds of small lights set into the decorative plaster-work illuminate the vast expanses of the sanctuary, the gorgeously painted ceiling, the elegant calligraphy, and other Islamic motifs.

At 575 feet (172.5 m) the minaret is both the tallest structure in the country and the tallest minaret in the world. It is surmounted by a dome that adds another 120 feet (36 m), and above that an arrow that pierces three golden globes of descending size. The mosque was built almost entirely from Moroccan materials, and more than 6,000 craftsmen took part in fashioning this monument to traditional Moroccan architecture.

"[Allah's] Throne was upon the water." This quotation from the Koran inspired the choice of location for the Hassan II Mosque, which sits on a platform built out over the sea.

Minarets stand out on the skyline of Fès.

FÈS, CITY OF MINARETS

Oxford, England, is known as the city of dreaming spires. Morocco's Fès could equally be dubbed the city of minarets. Each of these characteristically slim, square towers indicates the presence of a mosque and underlines the city's role as the country's Islamic heartland.

Fès is the most ancient of Morocco's four imperial cities. Its site—a long, flat valley enclosed by ranges of hills and bisected by a small river—was chosen in the late eighth century by Moulay Idriss I, the first Arab to establish wide-ranging and effective control in Morocco by subduing previously unconquered Berber tribes and converting them to Islam.

Within 50 years of its founding, Fès became home to two groups of Muslim refugees, the first from Cordoba in Andalusian Spain and the second from Kairouan in Tunisia. At the time these were the two most important cities in western Islam, and the commercial acumen and cultural skills the refugees brought with them had an enormous impact on the new city. Houses, shops, public baths, and flour mills were built on both sides of the river and merchants traveled from far and wide to buy and sell in the busy markets.

Two great mosques, the Karaouiyine and the Andalous, with their associated student colleges and residences, were the main focus of the city's religious life and masterpieces of Islamic architecture of the period. These institutions developed as places not only of prayer but also of religious knowledge, in addition to the study of mathematics, philosophy, and medicine.

In 1958–59 the Karaouiyine Mosque, now acknowledged as one of the oldest universities in the world, celebrated its 11th centenary. During the Middle Ages, the university had a great reputation as a center of Islamic culture. By the 14th century, it had 8,000 students. The university still functions today but most of its faculty and students have moved to more convenient premises outside the *medina*. The mosque, however, still remains the mecca of Morocco's religious life and its officials govern, for example, the timing of Ramadan and other Islamic festivals.

At the height of its power, at the beginning of the 13th century, Fès boasted 785 mosques for 125,000 inhabitants—roughly one mosque for every 170 people. Today a mosque is a legal requirement in each of the 187 different *quartiers* of Fès el Bali—the original old town—but the law is hardly necessary because the city still has no fewer than 300 mosques. It also has Morocco's most sacred saintly shrine—the *zaouia* erected in memory of Moulay Idriss II. By all accounts he was not a particularly saintly man but is revered as the sultan responsible for the development of Fès and as the son of the founder of the Arab Moroccan state.

Fès is three cities in one. In the 13th century, when old Fès was bulging to capacity within its walls, New Fès—Fès el Djedid—was built close by on slightly higher ground. It is a totally different city, characterized by wide, open spaces, splendid palaces, and military and administrative buildings. In the 20th century the French built a new town some distance outside the two ancient Fès cities.

LANGUAGE

MOROCCO'S OFFICIAL LANGUAGE is Arabic, but Arabic is not its only language. An individual Moroccan, for example, may well have Berber, Arab, Spanish, sub-Saharan, and Jewish blood. The country's languages reflect this heritage.

The vast majority of Moroccans are Arabized Berbers, that is, Muslim Berbers who have been strongly influenced by Arab culture and lifestyle. Around two-thirds of the population have Arabic as their first language and speak varying amounts of one of the local Berber languages. Among the Berbers who live in remote areas, Berber is the language of daily life.

The presence of the French during the Protectorate period also means that French has a high profile as a second language.

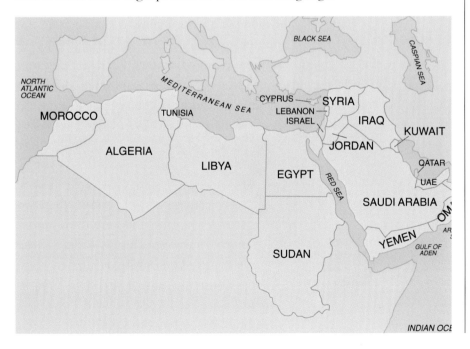

Left: **Countries where Arabic is the official language. It is estimated that about 60 million people from the countries of North Africa, across most of the Arabian peninsula, and as far east as Syria and Iraq have Arabic as their mother tongue. A much larger number—around 150 million—understand, read, or write it as their language of trade or the language of their religion. The Koran—Islam's equivalent of the Bible—is written in Arabic and recited in Arabic by all Muslims.**

Opposite: **Muslim schoolboys holding up religious placards written in Arabic in Fès.**

ARABIC MOROCCAN STYLE

Modern written Arabic is by and large the language of the Koran modified for use in modern times, so it is the same all over the world.

Written Arabic is the same for all Arabic speakers across the world. The spoken language, however, differs from country to country. The Arabic dialect spoken in Morocco is known as Darija.

In countries that are far apart, the differences can be enormous and

individual dialects mutually unintelligible. For instance, an Iraqi may find it difficult to communicate with a Moroccan, but since the Moroccan dialect is similar to that of Algeria and Tunisia, inhabitants of these three neighboring countries can generally understand each other.

One of the problems resulting from the numerous dialects of Arabic is that any one word may be pronounced in many different ways. As a consequence, phonetic spellings or transliterations of Arabic words vary. A case in point is *b'stilla* (bis-TEEL-ya), Morocco's famous pigeon pie, which may be pronounced as *pasteeya*, *bisteeya*, *bstila*, *pastilla*, *pastela*, and *bastela*. Nevertheless, there are a number of phrases that are understood wherever they are used across the entire Arabic-speaking world. These include *Insha'Allah* (in-SHAH-lah), or "God willing," and the formal greeting *Salaam oualeikum* (sa-LAAM wa-LAY-koom), meaning "Peace be with you."

Most Berbers know some Arabic.

BERBER LANGUAGES

There is no one standard Berber language but rather a group of languages spoken by separate Berber communities in various parts of North Africa. Moroccan Berbers speak one of three languages. Tarafit (also known as Rifia) is common among the inhabitants of the Rif Mountains in the north and parts of the Middle Atlas range. Other Middle Atlas tribes speak Tamazight, as do some High Atlas dwellers, while the language in other parts of the High Atlas, the southernmost valleys, and the Anti-Atlas, is Chleuh. For Chleuh speakers, Rifia is virtually a foreign language.

Since there is no standard Berber language, no universally accepted Berber script has evolved. There was a time when a few individual Berber languages were written in their own ancient script, as in the case of the Tuareg tribes in the Sahara Desert, but except for a few inscriptions, the Berber languages have practically no written literature. Today Arabic script is used for writing all the surviving Berber languages.

In Morocco, monolingual Berber speakers are now a minority. Most Berbers, except the most isolated, can understand some Arabic and use Arabic script for written communication among themselves.

OTHER LANGUAGES

Many English words have Arabic origins. Among the best-known are: "cipher," "algebra," "alcove," "alkali," "alcohol," "lemon," "sugar," "admiral," and "coffee."

With the exception of the very young and the very isolated, most Moroccans speak at least a smattering of French. This is a legacy of the Protectorate period, when French was established as the language of learning. The language is taught, even today, in the tiniest schools in the loneliest locations. The best educated are fluent French speakers.

Evidence of the prior French presence in Morocco is visible, and audible, at every turn. The months of the year are *Janvier, Février, Mars*, and so on, as in French, and traffic direction signs are invariably in both Arabic and French. Street names, especially in the cities, are frequently in both languages. French is also the language of business, and this enables Moroccans to communicate easily with the outside world, and particularly with European countries, which are Morocco's major trading partners.

Arabic script lends itself to decorative uses.

Following Moroccan independence, Spanish has not fared as well as French. Many inhabitants of the old Spanish Zone in the north—the Rif mountain range and the narrow strip along the Mediterranean coast as far as the Algerian border—still speak Spanish, but their numbers are dwindling. French is now the main second language in this once Spanish-dominated part of the country. Meanwhile English has been introduced as a second foreign language in secondary schools and at higher education levels. The purpose is to facilitate participation in international trade, which is increasingly in English, and to improve communication with English-speaking tourists, whose presence is becoming an important part of the Moroccan economy.

THE MEDIA

Moroccans have a choice of eight Arabic-language daily newspapers, in addition to five others published in French. There are also numerous periodicals in Arabic that deal with economic and political events. For a country with a relatively low literacy rate, this is a remarkable number of choices. In effect, however, independent comment is not as wide-ranging as one would expect, because the most important publications voice the government or establishment point of view or are linked to particular political parties.

The most important daily newspapers are the Arabic language *Al-Anba'a*, meaning "Information," and *Maroc Soir* and *Le Matin du Sahara*, which are both in French. These publications tend to support the establishment.

Electronic media present an alternative to this. While most Moroccans do not have a home computer, Internet access via cafés is widespread throughout the country and there is no effective censorship. This has given Moroccans the same freedom of access to information that is enjoyed by most people in the developed world.

Nearly all Moroccans spend a good deal of time listening to the radio. There are broadcasts in Arabic, French, and all the Berber dialects, featuring music and information. Talk radio is also an option. A television set is relatively expensive for the average Moroccan's budget, but they are gradually becoming more widespread. Anyone who can afford a television set can probably afford a satellite dish, and this gives Moroccans access to broadcasts from Europe and the rest of the Arab world. Most Moroccans welcome the variety this provides, but there are many programs that make parents feel uneasy because they threaten traditional values.

ARTS

THE LABYRINTHINE MAZES of the *medinas* enclose unique architectural jewels, and Morocco has a vital heritage of arts and crafts that is gaining international recognition. Moroccans also have a rich tradition of music and dance. Their classical music draws on Andalusian and Arab sources and includes religious music totally different in character from the religious music of the Christian world. Popular music in Morocco has borrowed modern instruments and themes from the West but continues to derive most of its inspiration from closer to home. Since independence, artists have begun to develop a repertoire of arts such as drama, sculpture, and painting.

The country's arts and crafts and architecture are extremely important to the economy. Moroccans are beginning to realize the importance of their artistic heritage and to take steps to protect it.

Left: **Pottery is a Moroccan specialty.**

Opposite: **The production of handicrafts employs over 7 percent of the Moroccan workforce.**

ARCHITECTURE

The Arabs who brought Islam to Morocco and converted the indigenous Berbers to their new religion also introduced a wealth of ideas about architecture and decorative techniques. As the centuries went by, successive sultans, both Berber and Arab, constructed mosques, *medersas*, minarets, and other buildings connected with religious practice, as well as palaces and public buildings to reflect their temporal power.

Architectural achievements in Morocco, however, are not mere copies of monuments that can be found elsewhere. The vast forests of oak, pine, and cedar allowed local artisans to develop a tradition of decorative woodcarving, and the absence of abundant supplies of precious metals led them to apply their creative skills to stucco and ceramic mosaic.

Both of these materials and the techniques for using them were Eastern in origin, but were perfected in Andalusian Spain. They came to Morocco by way of Moorish refugees from the Christian reconquest of the country. The refugees also brought with them the tradition of domes, pillars, and semicircular and horseshoe arches.

The builders of Moroccan mosques were inspired by the great mosques of Kairouan in Tunisia and Cordoba in Spain. Moroccan mosques are unadorned on the outside and their roofs are covered in plain green tiles. But in contrast to the austere simplicity of the exterior the entrance is a highly decorated door that leads into paved

Bahia Palace in Marrakech. The wealthy built themselves personal oases filled with beauty and hidden away from the heat, dust, and hubbub of the outside world.

THE WRITING ON THE WALL

Islam discourages pictorial representation of living things and prohibits any representation of God. This is one of the reasons why Arabic script has been raised to the level of an art form. Arabic writing is quintessentially elegant and offers enormous scope for imaginative presentation in rectangular, circular, and oblong shapes, and in the forms of fruit and birds, buildings and stars, lamps, and a host of other configurations. It also lends itself to use on a wide variety of materials from paper and stone to stucco, ceramic, glass, wood, metal, ivory, and fabric. Within a religious building, it is most often used for naming Allah and his attributes and for the decorative presentation of verses of the Koran.

courtyards where fountains play and walls are covered with green, blue, red, and black mosaics and expanses of exquisitely patterned stucco. Doors, window frames, and screens are carved in patterns so delicate that they look like lace, and frieze after frieze carries calligraphic inscriptions and bands of intertwined foliage, flowers, and geometric patterns. Towering above all this ornamentation is the square minaret so characteristic of the Maghreb countries.

Palaces and other major buildings also feature the same lively and open Islamic styles with their emphasis on space.

PROTECTING ONESELF

In the south in particular, tribal warfare and the struggles of emerging dynasties produced architecture with defense as its prime objective. Examples of this form of architecture range from tall, crenellated, fortified houses and villages to cities encircled by massive walls pierced by gates of monumental proportions.

In the countryside and desert areas, construction materials were rudimentary and of poor quality—crudely made unfired bricks and plaster—but the buildings were often adorned with geometric decorations carved into the mud or onto the rough wood of the doors. This decorative tradition has continued to the present, although the doors are now metal and paint is widely available. Windows are carefully embellished with ornamentation ranging from crude daubings to the pretty wrought-iron grilles inspired by Moorish Spain. At the same time, much of the decoration in areas close to the Sahara reveal Morocco's contacts with the totally different world of sub-Saharan Africa.

The ramparts of the *kasbah* in Rabat show crenellated walls with a large *bab*, or gate.

The great walled cities were intended not only to defend a tribe or a dynasty but also to reflect their builder's wealth, success, and power. This was sometimes short-lived, especially when successors or rivals destroyed what previous sultans had constructed. The city walls were high, crenelated, thick, and usually plain, but their huge *babs*, or gateways, were an opportunity for sumptuous decoration and ostentatious display of wealth. They were generally built of stone and had a central archway, sometimes flanked by crenellated towers.

BAB EL MANSOUR

The Bab el Mansour in Meknès is the finest of Morocco's collection of city gates. It is immense, perfectly proportioned, and richly decorated with green and white ceramics. The central bay, where the gateway itself is set, is flanked by squat bastions similarly decorated and partly supported by elegant marble columns. The decoration is based on a traditional pattern called *darj w ktarf*, meaning "cheek and shoulder." The mosaic work is elaborate and richly colored. There are also layers of cut-away black tiles. The ornamental inscriptions surmounting the whole include the claim that there is no gate in the Islamic world of the 17th century that can be called its equal.

RELAXATION

Another of the many artistic ideas that Morocco gleaned from its links with Spain and the Middle East is that of the formal, but restful, garden with its greenery, fountains, and running water. These gardens are quiet havens where women come to meet while their children play. Park benches are filled with students deep in study, while members of the older generation skim through the newspaper or snooze in the sun.

The capital, Rabat, has a delightful walled Andalusian garden. It was constructed by the French in the first half of the 20th century but is called "Andalusian" because its design is so faithful to the ancient Spanish garden tradition. Beds of hibiscus, roses, lilies, marigolds, poinsettias, and sweet-smelling herbs are separated by straight paths and, as in all of Morocco's parks, the garden is usually filled with pedestrians.

Many cities today have shady parks where the air is filled with the scent of orange blossoms, and the lilac flowers of the jacarandas vie with the blue of the North African sky.

CARPETS, KILIMS, *AND SILVER*

Traditional handicrafts include rugs, carpets, metalwork, jewelry, leather goods, woodwork, and pottery. Of these, the most important are Morocco's colorful knotted carpets and woven rugs. Carpets from Rabat are generally acknowledged as the finest and most valuable. Their design— a central medallion and a wide border with an intricate pattern— is Turkish in origin and was introduced in the 18th century.

The woven *kilims,* or rugs, made by various Berber tribes are quite different, and designs are passed from one generation to the next. It is claimed that a glance at the pattern and the colors used will reveal at least the region, possibly the tribe, and in some cases the individual family that produced the rug.

Middle Atlas *kilims* are mostly worked in beiges and browns. In the High Atlas reds and ochres predominate, whereas in the area around Ouarzazate reds and blues figure prominently. Some rugs are finely worked in a combination of wool and silk, many are quite thin and the best are hung in tents or on the wall rather than put on the floor.

Metalwork similarly ranges from the simple and utilitarian to the delicate and decorative. The metalworking *souks* reverberate to the beating of copper and brass and to the gentle tap of the jeweler's hammer. Artisans transform silver into incised teapots and trays, daggers and scabbards,

Rugs are an important handicraft in Morocco.

JEWELRY FOR ALL OCCASIONS

Whatever their means or status, Moroccan women wear jewelry as a matter of course. A countrywoman bent double under a load of firewood may well be wearing a heavy silver chain decorated with old coins or a necklace of chunky amber beads. Her more sophisticated sister in town may choose a more contemporary style, but nonetheless she is likely to be adorned at least with a necklace, ring, and earrings, and possibly with bracelets and pins as well.

In some cases, decoration goes beyond mere adornment. Tattoos on the hands or faces of some Berber women are intended to ward off illness or misfortune. Silver "hands of Fatima" (Fatima was the Prophet Mohammed's daughter) are worn as pendants for the same purpose. However, the protection given by a certain type of large bracelet with protruding knobs is different. These bracelets, or so the story goes, are actually used by their wearers for physical self-defense.

Koran boxes with intricate silver-wire decorations, and, above all, the bracelets, necklaces, pins, and pendants with which Moroccan women love to adorn themselves.

Morocco's abundant sheep and goats provide a source of skins for the leather trade, and "bound in Morocco" has long been a phrase used to indicate the good quality of a book's binding. Moroccan leather has also been used for centuries to make sandals and saddlebags and especially the distinctive pointed slippers known as *bilgha* (bil-GHAH) that are worn in various forms by most Moroccan men and many Moroccan women.

Woodworking is another Moroccan craft that has survived the march of mechanized progress. Local woodworkers produce a variety of items from simple, utilitarian dishes and boxes to painted and carved chairs and tables. Some of their handiwork is painstakingly inlaid with contrasting veneers or mother-of-pearl.

Potters in Fès, Meknès, Marrakech, and Safi have built upon a reputation that goes back many centuries. They produce simple but colorful pottery and are best known for their boldly patterned bowls and serving dishes.

105

MUSIC

The most widely heard modern music is *chabbi*, which means "popular." It is often played in cafés, many of which keep instruments specifically for the musicians who come to sip a glass of tea and then launch into a jam session. *Chabbi* began as music performed by traveling entertainers who collected and composed songs as they went along. In recent times, it is no longer confined to impromptu performances in public squares. The best groups now perform regularly on radio and television.

This kind of music is a mixture of Arab, African, and Western styles. It also includes elements from traditional Berber music, Arabic poetry, and ritual religious music, and is played by musicians who work together like a Western group. At the end of a song, however, an instrumental section is sometimes played at double speed so that the audience bursts into shouting, dancing, and syncopated clapping.

Another form of modern music called *rai* (rye)—performed rock-style and backed by electric instruments—has lyrics that focus on such topics as sex, alcohol, drugs, and cars, and is not popular in conservative parts of Moroccan society.

The day is punctuated by the call of the muezzin *reminding Muslims of their obligation to pray. His chanting voice, tinnily amplified, rings out from a loudspeaker on the minaret that towers above streets and homes.*

COUNTRY STYLE

Among the Berber tribes, especially where the illiteracy rate is high, music and dancing play an important role in community life because they are often the strongest form of self-expression. Some forms of Berber music involve the whole village in circular dances and a kind of chanted singing. The women hold hands and move in slow circles around the drummers, who crouch close to the flames of a glowing fire that tightens the skins on the drums. It is rhythmic, compelling music and is usually performed on a festive occasion or in honor of visitors or guests.

The Berbers also have special ritual music for important lifetime events such as a marriage, or for an exorcism or purification ceremony. And in days not so long ago the majority of rural people received information about events outside their immediate circle from professional musicians who traveled from village to village singing the news. These *imdyazn* (IM-dee-AZN), as they are called, have largely been put out of business by radio and television.

Morocco's equivalent of the classical music of the West developed from

A performance of a traditional dance.

songs and music introduced by Arabs from the East and refugees from Andalusia. It is generally played by one of the country's three most important orchestras, which are based in Fès, Meknès, and Tangier—the cities most profoundly influenced by Moorish Spain.

LEISURE

LEISURE PURSUITS IN MOROCCO are a mixture of simple and traditional entertainment for the majority, with a few sophisticated and more expensive activities for the well-to-do. Some of the latter activities are Moroccan in origin, but others were introduced by foreigners during the Protectorate period. In addition, certain sports are being actively developed because of their potential for attracting tourists.

The way people spend their leisure time depends on where they live, their position in society, and their economic circumstances. The poor often do not have a lot of spare time, although in farming and nomadic communities there may be periods of intense activity followed by periods with little to do. But if you live far from civilization, if your home lacks a basic amenity such as electricity, or if you cannot read, then most of your leisure time is probably occupied by chatting with your neighbors, playing traditional games, or listening to a battery-powered radio. On special occasions—holidays or the arrival of a visitor—there may be celebrations with music and dancing.

Town and city dwellers, especially those who are financially better off, have more choices. These could include a visit to the movies or a swimming pool—municipal pools are quite common—or an afternoon at a soccer match, soccer being the national sport. Other possibilities are a visit to the beach for those who live near the coast or watching television, if it is available. Men often take advantage of the television sets that flicker in the corner of many cafés.

For a privileged few there is golf, hunting, shooting, and fishing, as well as water sports at many resorts.

Opposite: **A rural Berber takes time to prepare a leisurely cup of tea.**

Below: **Movie theaters are mostly for men. Popular fare includes Indian films and adventure movies.**

ENTERTAINMENT MOROCCAN STYLE

For Moroccans, a great deal of leisure is genuinely leisurely in nature. Living life to the fullest does not necessarily mean cramming activity into every spare moment, and a great deal of leisure is family oriented. Eating out is not common, but eating well is much enjoyed. Most people place great emphasis in eating good food at home in the convivial presence of family and friends and welcome an excuse for a *diffa*, or banquet, however simple it may be.

Similarly, families go out together. The evening promenade is especially popular in summer. In big cities smartly dressed locals frequent the cafés on the shady boulevards and watch the world go by. In less sophisticated places, women and children enjoy an excursion to a park or some other shady spot, while many men tend to congregate in cafés to discuss local affairs and exchange gossip over coffee or mint tea.

Evening is the time for window-shopping. In the *medinas*, shoppers throng the streets when the shutters are removed after the afternoon siesta, the streets come alive, and the markets truly buzz with activity.

TRADITIONAL ENTERTAINMENT

Part of the fun of the evening promenade is the chance of seeing any one of dozens of different kinds of itinerant entertainers. These include storytellers and magicians, acrobats, jugglers and dancers, musicians and singers, snake charmers with mesmerized and mesmerizing reptiles, and tame monkeys taught to perform tricks.

The Djemm el'Fna in Marrakech, in particular, is famed for the array of traditional entertainers who appear at dusk. Crowds drift from one group or stall to another, and there is continuous pulsating activity. Storytellers attract large circles of listeners. Tumblers, acrobats, and skillful jugglers weave their way through the audience as it ebbs and flows. Gaudily dressed watersellers festooned with brass cups ring their bells insistently, adding to the din of singers, the blare of pop music, musicians playing reed pipes, and drummers beating out wild rhythms, some of which can induce a trance.

Special outings usually take the form of a trip to a *moussem* (MOO-sem), a festival in honor of a local saint. These are enormously joyful occasions with a country-fair atmosphere.

A visit to a hammam, *or public bath, can be a necessity for those who do not have running water in their homes. For others it may be primarily a social occasion. Every* medina *has its* hammam *with plentiful supplies of hot water and sometimes opportunities for an invigorating massage. Bathing is strictly segregated, and modesty is important. Both men and women wear underwear. Some* hammams *are for one sex only; at others, men and women have different hours.*

THE SPORTING LIFE

The national sport is soccer, but there is increasing interest in a range of other sports such as tennis and swimming. To some extent this new interest is driven by economic concerns. Tourism is one of Morocco's biggest hard-currency earners. Morocco can offer sports-minded visitors golf, water sports, hunting, shooting, fishing, and adventure vacations, while the influx of visitors boosts employment in many depressed areas.

Farmers, for example, and others living in places where the scenery is dramatic and exotic, benefit from the demand for outdoor vacations. On the coasts, vast stretches of beach in generally unproductive areas are being developed as seaside resorts.

SOCCER

Morocco has appeared four times in the World Cup competition: 1970, 1986, 1994, and 1998. Their players have gained the respect of the international soccer community with each successive appearance. Morocco has bid to host the World Cup competition four times but has not yet succeeded. They hosted the African Cup of Nations in 1988, and will try to do so again in 2010.

GOLFING THE ROYAL WAY

Although soccer is the national obsession, golf has a longer history in Morocco. The first course opened in Tangier in 1917 and was primarily used by the diplomatic community in the international zone. Nevertheless, several more courses, mostly in the central areas and main cities, opened even before independence.

During the reign of King Hassan II, who was an avid golfer, the sport increased tremendously in popularity. It is significant that the word "Royal" features in the name of many clubs. The 1980s and 1990s have seen courses increase in number and improve dramatically in quality. This has a lot to do with royal patronage and the realization that golf can play a prominent role in attracting the kind of wealthy tourists that the country seeks. It is hoped that the prospect of perfect playing weather nearly all year round, good courses and facilities, and reasonable course and caddy fees will prove irresistible attractions for dedicated golfers.

Morocco's best soccer teams are FAR, which is drawn from armed forces personnel, WIDAD and RAJA, which are both Casablanca-based, MAS from Fès, and KAC from Kénitra.

OTHER SPORTS

Ordinary Moroccans have access to public swimming pools, and the country's long coastline provides ample opportunity to enjoy other water sports, such as windsurfing, sailing, and diving. At present, these are expensive in Moroccan terms, but they will slowly become more accessible to a larger proportion of the population.

Another sport with an expensive image is skiing, but a number of ski resorts have operated in the Atlas Mountains for several years and are well patronized by local enthusiasts in the closest towns—Fès, Meknès, and Rabat—and by youth clubs and schools. Slopes and lodge facilities do not compare in quality with those in the United States or Europe, but cross-country skiing has great potential.

FESTIVALS

MOROCCO HAS A PLETHORA of festivals and holidays. Some are celebrated on a national scale, and many are regional or local occasions. Four major festivals are directly connected with important religious events or dates. In addition, there are a myriad of *moussems*, which are primarily festivals connected with the cult of a local saint or holy man.

Regardless of whether they are secular or religious in character, Moroccan festivals are joyous affairs, marked by music, dancing, feasting, and a good deal of commercial activity as well. The newer state holidays also tend to incorporate parades and official ceremonies.

Most of the secular holidays have come into being since the country became independent in 1956. The most important of them is the Festival of the Throne—the anniversary of the accession of King Mohammed VI in 1999. It is sometimes called Throne Day and is marked countrywide by fireworks, parades, music, and dancing often lasting considerably longer than one day. Green March Remembrance Day commemorates the march into Western Sahara in 1975.

Opposite: **Berber women participating in a traditional marriage *moussem*, or festival, in the High Atlas.**

FIXED OFFICIAL STATE HOLIDAYS

January 1	New Year's Day
July 30	Festival of the Throne
May 1	Labor Day
August 14	Allegiance Day
August 20	Revolution of the King and the People
November 6	Green March Remembrance Day
November 18	Independence Day

RELIGIOUS CELEBRATIONS AND HOLIDAYS

A sheep for Aïd el Kebir. The animals are bought well in advance so that they can be fattened up. They are tethered wherever there is space, often on the flat roofs of the houses.

Morocco's major religious holidays—Aïd es Seghir, Aïd el Kebir, Muharram, and Aïd Mouloud—have long histories going back to the arrival of Islam. They fall on different dates each year because they are linked to the Islamic lunar calendar rather than the Gregorian solar calendar.

Aïd es Seghir is the celebration that marks the end of Ramadan, the fasting month similar in concept to the Christian Lent. The festival effectively brings Morocco to a standstill for two days, although feasting and rejoicing often continue for up to a week. Special food is prepared well in advance, and new clothes are bought for the occasion.

Aïd el Kebir commemorates Abraham's willingness to sacrifice his son, Isaac, if God so commanded. Like Aïd es Seghir, it is traditionally a family gathering. For Aïd el Kebir, every household that can afford to do so slaughters a sheep. After the feast the skins can be seen being cured in the streets.

The first day of the month of Muharram is a one-day festival to mark the Islamic New Year, but festivities for Aïd Mouloud—the birthday of the Prophet Mohammed—extend over two days. A large number of *moussems* also occur in the weeks before and after the prophet's birthday.

A celebration for Aïd el Kebir, the holiday when Muslims make the pilgrimage to Mecca.

THE ISLAMIC CALENDAR

The Islamic calendar is a lunar system consisting of 12 months, each starting at the new moon. Alternate months have 29 or 30 days except the last, Dhu al-Hijjah (DOO al-HEE-jah), the length of which varies over a 30-year period to keep the calendar in step with the phases of the moon. For 11 years of the cycle this month has 30 days, and the following year it has 29. An Islamic year therefore numbers 354 or 355 days and is about 11 days shorter than the solar year. It is for this reason that the dates of the religious festivals vary. For example, in 1994 Aïd Seghir was celebrated on March 12, whereas 10 years later, in 2004, it took place on November 15. In general, religious holidays take place about 10 days earlier than they did the previous year, and are not known precisely in advance. This lack of certainty occurs because the actual date is determined by the sighting of the new moon.

Years are reckoned from A.D. 622—the date of the Hegira, when opposition to his radical new ideas forced Mohammed to flee from his home in Mecca. Because the lunar year of the Islamic calendar is shorter than the solar year of the Gregorian calendar, the two systems never coincide. The year 2005 corresponds to 1426 in the Islamic calendar.

Ramadan is a time for self-denial mixed with restrained celebration. In the daytime Moroccans abstain from all food and drink but at sunset there is a sense of happy relief as everyone hurries home to satisfy their hunger and slake their thirst. The evenings and nights are spent in prayer, joyful feasting, and relaxation before the fast begins as daylight reappears.

117

While singing, dancing, and general merrymaking are the order of the day, if conditions and cost permit, the highlight of moussem *celebrations will be a dramatic* fantasia. *Horsemen brandishing rifles gallop at full speed across an open space, firing their weapons into the air as they go. The horses and their nobly dressed riders dash past, and the air is filled with swirling dust and sand, whoops, shouts, gunfire, and contagious excitement.*

MOUSSEM *MERRYMAKING*

Moussems are primarily local events. They vary widely in their form, purpose, and style, and are the staples of festive life in rural areas.

There are an enormous number of *moussems*. A few have developed into substantial occasions, and one or two have become tourist attractions. Some are little more than once-a-year markets with tenuous religious connections, whereas others are harvest festivals.

The dates of individual *moussems* vary from year to year for two main reasons. Harvest festivals depend on the weather and the harvest being complete, whereas religious *moussems* are linked to the lunar calendar. Thus their dates move, just as the dates of Aïd es Seghir and other Islamic festivals move each year.

Ostensibly, the main purpose of a *moussem* is to honor a local *marabout*, or holy man, generally in the immediate surroundings of his tomb, or *koubba*. These are usually small, white, domed buildings that can be seen dotted all over the countryside or, in cramped towns and cities, set between ordinary shops and houses. People come to the tomb in the hope of obtaining the *marabout's* blessing, to ask a favor, or, in the case of harvest festivals, to give thanks for what Allah has provided.

THE MAJOR *MOUSSEMS*

Some *moussems* have grown so large that the traditional focus—devotion to the *marabout*—has become obscured. The greatest and grandest of the *moussems*, and one regularly attended by the king, is held in honor of Moulay Idriss at Meknès. However, despite much holiday-type activity, it is still an intensely religious event. Conversely, at Imilchil in the eastern High Atlas Mountains, the "marriage" *moussem*—sometimes known as the Brides Festival—is like a county show or state fair and is fast becoming a tourist event.

Families and communities from remote areas ride to a *moussem* on their donkeys and horses.

Families travel from far and wide to attend. Buses may bring groups, but individual families and small communities from remote spots come on foot or ride in on their donkeys or mules. Tents are pitched, carpets laid on the ground, vegetables and produce set out, and the festivities get under way.

Every *moussem* has a strong social dimension. The gatherings are also extremely colorful events. Most rural people, particularly the women, still wear local dress. A *moussem* is an opportunity to dress up in one's best clothes and put on one's finest jewelry. More important from a social point of view, perhaps, is that family members and relatives scattered in different villages can reunite, and marriages can be arranged. Politics and family matters are also discussed, information about current events and prices gets passed around, and the community dances, sings, eats, and prays together.

FOOD

MOROCCO'S FOOD IS EXOTIC, rich in its variety, and until recent times virtually unknown in the outside world. The development of Morocco's unique cuisine has been made possible by the availability of a wealth of good ingredients, and food traditions introduced by successive waves of invaders from the north and south and, most importantly, from the east.

The agricultural areas of Morocco produce numerous fruits and vegetables: oranges, lemons, pomegranates, melons, tomatoes, sweet and hot peppers, edible gourds, potatoes, almonds, olives, and figs. Fish and seafood abound on the coast, while climate and pasture in many areas enable flocks of sheep and goats to thrive. Even the desert supplies a rich harvest of dates from its remote oases.

Some of these items have always been available in Morocco and were used by the indigenous Berbers in the preparation of long-simmered stews of lamb, poultry, and vegetables and other traditional dishes. Various invaders introduced a number of now traditional ingredients, along with previously unknown preparation and cooking methods.

The Arabs introduced spices, various types of bread, and dishes based on grain products, as well as delicious pastries. Meanwhile, contact with the sophisticated society of Andalusia in southern Spain taught Moroccan cooks to experiment with olives and olive oil, and combinations of fruits, nuts, and herbs in cooked dishes. In modern times, the French and even the British have also made their contributions.

Below: **The Phoenicians brought exotic spices to Morocco, as did traders from Senegal traveling from the south across the Sahara, and Arabs from the Middle East. Today no town is without its spice shop and no market lacks a stall dedicated to the sale of cinnamon, saffron, cumin, and numerous other spices.**

Opposite: **The open-air food stalls of Djemm el'Fna are world famous; the entire square was designated by UNESCO as one of the masterpieces of the oral and intangible heritage of humanity.**

STAPLES: BREAD AND TAJINE

Flat, round, chewy bread, freshly baked every day, is very much the staff of life in Morocco. Folklore and various sayings underline its value and the almost religious significance with which it is regarded. For many poor people, bread combined with a few olives or dates, or perhaps a small piece of cheese, and washed down with a glass of hot mint tea, is a meal in itself.

Tajine in a restaurant. Sizes of *tajine* pots vary from small dishes for one person to dishes of mammoth proportions that can hold enough food for 20 people.

Bread is eaten at every meal. It is cut in wedges and used both as an accompaniment to whatever food is being served and as a kind of fork or spoon. Crusty chunks are particularly useful for scooping up meat and vegetables and for mopping up the tasty sauces of Morocco's many *tajine* (ta-JEEN) stews. These are casseroles of meat and poultry named after the cooking pot in which they are cooked. *Tajine* pots are generally made from earthenware and are used on charcoal braziers. They consist of a flat dish with a rim and a conical lid that fits into the dish.

The most common *tajine* recipes are based on lamb or chicken cut into segments and marinated in olive oil with chopped onion and garlic. Various combinations of saffron, cumin, and crushed red pepper, in addition to fresh coriander and parsley, are added to give extra flavor. The meat is first sautéed and then simmered in the marinade until it is tender.

Depending on the recipe, the meat may be combined with prunes or almonds, tomatoes, vegetables, and hard-boiled eggs. A distinctive dish combines chicken, olives, and salted lemons. In cases where meat is not available or is too expensive, *tajines* are made from vegetables alone.

THE NATIONAL DISH

Although a Moroccan family may eat several *tajines* every week, the title of national dish goes to couscous—cream-colored grains of semolina steamed over a highly flavored stock made from meat and vegetables and served with the meat and a sauce made from the bouillon.

Like *tajine*, couscous has two meanings. The word refers to the semolina itself and to the cooked dish. No one knows exactly where the name comes from, but one amusing suggestion is that it is an attempt to imitate the hissing sound that occurs when steam is forced through the holes in the steamer—the couscoussier—in which the grains are cooked.

The dish is so popular that one could say there are as many types of couscous as there are cooks. Some make a simple dish with vegetables and chickpeas. Others make it with meat, lamb, chicken, or sometimes rabbit or pigeon.

There are couscous dishes with dates and raisins, highly seasoned varieties, and plain varieties served with a spicy red pepper sauce.

OLIVES AND LEMONS

A variety of olives, and lemons pickled in lemon juice and salt, are essential ingredients in many dishes. The lemons are sold loose or packed in jars. The preserving gives the skins a silken texture and a unique flavor.

Olives come in a variety of flavors, colors, and sizes. Some stalls sell nothing but olives: bitter, unripe green olives, riper olives ranging from tan and russet through violet, and fully ripe, cured black olives.

123

A shop selling traditional sweet pastries at a *souk* in Marrakech.

B'STILLA

In times of rejoicing, Moroccans are likely to celebrate with a banquet featuring one of their most famous dishes—*b'stilla*.

B'stilla is usually presented as a spectacular first course. It is made with an extravagant combination of highly spiced pigeon meat, creamy lemon-flavored eggs or hard-boiled eggs, and almonds. This is baked or fried in a circular case of overlapping leaves of thin pastry and topped with a lattice-like sugar and cinnamon decoration before serving.

The pastry, known as *warka* (WAH-kar), is a Moroccan version of the French *mille-feuille* (MEAL-fe-ye) pastry. The best *warka* is tissue-thin and so time-consuming to make that many Moroccans buy their supplies from Sudanese women who specialize in preparing it.

There are many regional versions of this dish. The classic *b'stilla* is said to come from Fès. Tétouan has a chicken-based version, and people living in the Middle Atlas Mountains sometimes use minced beef or lamb in place of pigeon. As with couscous, *b'stilla* can be sweet as well as spicy. In Rabat *b'stilla* filled with rice cooked in almond milk and scented with orange-flower water is served both as a first course and as a dessert. Similarly the inhabitants of Marrakech have developed *keneffa* (ken-EFF-ah)—a type of *b'stilla* with an orange-flavored custard filling.

BARBECUED WHOLE LAMB

If circumstances permit, *b'stilla* may be followed by *mechoui* (mesh-SHOE-ee)—charcoal roasted whole lamb, a Berber specialty. Lamb is the mainstay of Moroccan meat cooking. It is grilled as brochettes, minced for use as a stuffing for vegetables, and is one of the main ingredients in countless *tajine* and couscous recipes.

A lamb for *mechoui* is rubbed with garlic and spices and then cooked slowly on a spit over burning charcoal embers. It is basted regularly with herbal butter so that it becomes crisp on the outside and succulent underneath. The best *mechoui* is so tender that the crispy fat on the outside peels away easily and the meat breaks off in the hand. The roast meat is served with spices and plain bread.

CELEBRATING AÏD EL KEBIR

Mechoui is traditionally eaten during the Aïd el Kebir festival that takes place soon after the end of Ramadan. The festival commemorates Abraham's willingness to sacrifice his son, Isaac, in obedience to God's command. At the last moment, as Abraham prepared to kill Isaac, God provided a ram as a sacrifice in place of the child.

Those who cannot afford a whole lamb for this celebration, or who do not have the necessary large oven or spit for roasting out of doors, make do with a part of a lamb. The poorest Moroccans sometimes substitute roasted kid or maybe chicken.

PASTRIES

Moroccans are notorious for their love of sweet cakes, pastries, and desserts. Pastry shops are filled with goodies based on pounded almonds, dates, and figs, flavored with the distilled essence of orange blossom or rose petals, and soaked in honey. Little "lovers' cakes" are stuffed with dates or other tasty sweetmeats, and parcels of *warka* pastry with delicious fillings take a myriad of shapes. Some are long and thin like cigarettes. *Briouats* (BREE-oo-at) are triangular and are dipped in simmering honey. Special favorites are the crescent-shaped "gazelle's horn" pastries and the flat, baked rounds of "coiled serpent" cake. Both are stuffed with flavored almond paste and dusted with confectioners' sugar. No less sweet and tempting is *ktaif* (ke-TIE-ff) with its sheets of butter-fried pastry spread with a mixture of almonds, cinnamon, and confectioners' sugar moistened with orange-flower water.

Some of the many varieties of sweet Moroccan pastries.

In the days when spices and essences were expensive items, these mouthwatering delights were only available to sultans, caliphs, and the elite. Today sweet cakes are part and parcel of festive family occasions such as births and weddings, and are also served on a day-to-day basis, when neighbors and friends come together for a morning chat or afternoon break.

Sweet dishes, on the other hand, are special-occasion dishes and are normally served before the fresh fruit or fruit salads with which an important Moroccan meal concludes. Sweet couscous garnished with prunes, raisins, and decorative trails of powdered cinnamon and confectioners' sugar, the sweet *b'stilla* concoctions, and a rice pudding studded with sautéed pine nuts and raisins steeped in orange-flower water fall into this category. All are sweet, rich, and celebratory and make a fine contrast to the fruit and nuts that follow.

IN ADDITION TO TEA

Although mint-flavored green tea is the main Moroccan drink, it is by no means the only one. In season every town has stalls piled high with mounds of golden oranges and tempting glasses of juice on display. Drinks based on citrus fruits, pomegranates, and grapes are very popular. So too are *sharbats*—fruit- or nut-flavored milk drinks with shaved ice—and sharp, yogurt-based thirst-quenchers. Morocco also has its own widely available mineral waters as well as numerous sodas.

Café cassé (ka-FAY KA-say)—half-and-half black coffee and hot milk—served in small cups is widely drunk. *Café Ras el Hanout* (ka-FAY ras el ha-NOOT) is a spiced coffee. *Ras el Hanout* is a strong, ancient mixture of anywhere between 10 and 26 spices.

Watersellers in traditional, elaborate dress.

Wine is produced in vineyards first planted by the French, but most goes for export because devout Muslims do not drink alcohol.

EATING IN AND EATING OUT

Food and meals play an enormously important role in Moroccan family life. Cooking is regarded as an art, and family occasions—births, circumcisions, marriages, name days, and other events—are opportunities for a celebratory *diffa*, a banquet that may be quite extravagant.

Everyday meals are relatively simple. Again depending on circumstances, the main meal for an ordinary family on an ordinary day may be a simple *tajine*, with meat if finances allow, or a dish of couscous with vegetables and meat if available. Alternatively there could be a nourishing, thick soup. Either way, the main dish is served with large wedges of bread, possibly with fresh fruit to finish, and almost certainly with hot mint tea.

Traditionally, meals are served on low, usually round tables. Diners sit on cushions around the table and use the thumb and first two fingers of their right hands to serve themselves from a central dish. Occasionally a spoon is provided, but bread is by far the most widely used implement.

Food stalls provide tasty snacks: bowls of steaming soup, hot chickpeas or broad beans,

Left: **Dates for sale in a food market.**

Opposite: **Finally, to round off a banquet, there is, as always, freshly brewed mint tea.**

hard-boiled eggs dusted with cumin, meat grilled on skewers, simple salads, and sweet cakes. Freshly cooked ring doughnuts are threaded on string and carried home.

FOOD AS CHARITY

The Arabic word for charity is *sadaqa* (sah-DAK-ah), but in Morocco it has a special meaning with regard to food. On the 40th day after someone dies, or on a death anniversary, family members offer a special meal. This meal is called a *sadaqa* and its purpose is to honor the deceased by showing charity on their behalf. Charity, in the form of giving alms to the poor, is one of the Five Pillars of Islam, and charity in the form of a special meal is one way that Moroccan Muslims observe this aspect of their religion.

The people invited to a *sadaqa* are usually family members and friends of the family who knew the deceased, but the overriding idea of the meal is charity, and anyone who turns up will be offered food. In addition food from a *sadaqa* may be sent to neighbors or to others who are needy.

The food at a *sadaqa* is always special and delicious. Many different cakes and cookies with expensive ingredients are associated with the *sadaqa* and people always appreciate the opportunity to throw one or to eat at one.

MAAQODA (POTATO CROQUETTES)

This recipe serves four.

1½ pounds potatoes (or the same amount in leftover mashed potatoes)
2 cloves of garlic, crushed
½ tablespoon ground cumin
½ tablespoon ground paprika or chili
½ teaspoon turmeric

1 teaspoon salt
2 tablespoons fresh parsley, chopped
2 tablespoons fresh cilantro, chopped
2 eggs
oil

Boil the potatoes until their skins crack and they become tender. Peel and mash the potatoes, leaving some lumps (If leftover mashed potatoes are used, just use them at room temperature). Add the garlic, spices, salt, parsley, and cilantro to the mash and mix well. Mix in one egg. Heat the oil in a frying pan over medium heat. Form little cakes with the potato mixture. Beat the other egg in a shallow bowl. Coat the cakes in the beaten egg, then place the cakes into the hot oil. Fry for two minutes on each side. When the cakes are uniformly cooked, remove from the pan and put on paper towels. Serve warm.

HALIB B-LOOZ (ALMOND MILK)

This is one of the most refreshing and popular drinks in Morocco. It can be served as a dessert or afternoon snack.

1½ cups cold milk
½ cup blanched almonds, skinned
3 tablespoons sugar

Put all the ingredients in a blender. Blend until the almonds are completely ground and the mixture is uniform. Serve in tall glasses.

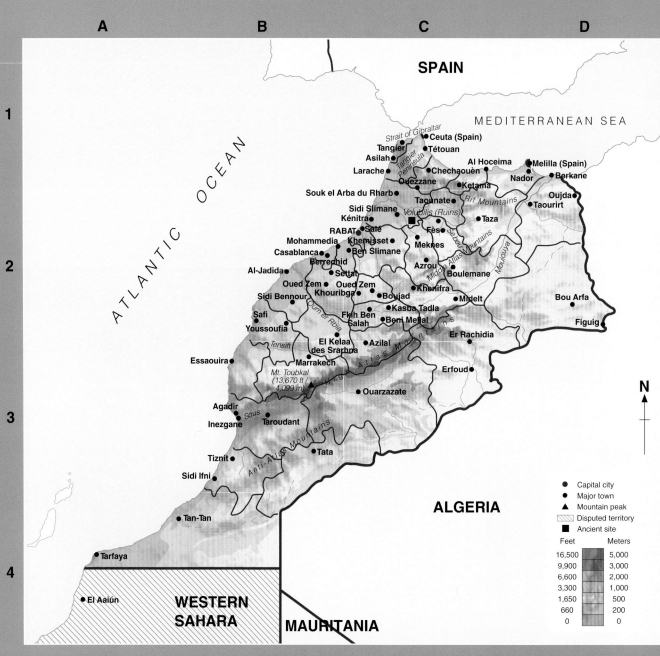

SPAIN

MEDITERRANEAN SEA

Strait of Gibraltar
Ceuta (Spain)
Tangier • •Tétouan
Asilah •
Al Hoceima
Melilla (Spain)•
Larache •Chechaouèn
Nador• •Berkane
Tangier Peninsula
Ouezzane
Souk el Arba du Rharb •
Ketama
Oujda•
Taounate •Taourirt
Sidi Slimane
Volubilis (Ruins)■
Rif Mountains
Kénitra •
•Taza
RABAT• •Salé
Fès •
Mohammedia •
Khemisset •
Meknes •
Casablanca •
Ben Slimane
Sebou Mountains
Berrechid •
Azrou •
Al-Jadida •
Settat •
Boulemane •
Middle Atlas Mountains
Oued Zem •
Oued Zem •
Sidi Bennour •
Khouribga •
Khenifra •
Moulouya
Safi •
Boujad •
Kasba Tadla •
Midelt •
Bou Arfa •
Youssoufia •
Flkh Ben Salah •
Beni Mellal •
Figuig•
Oum er Rbia
El Kelaa des Srarhna •
Azilal •
Er Rachidia •
Tensift
Essaouira •
Marrakech •
Mt. Toubkal (13,670 ft / 4,099 m) ▲
Atlas Mountains
Erfoud •
Ouarzazate •
Agadir •
Sous
Inezgane •
Taroudant •
Anti-Atlas Mountains
Tiznit •
Tata •
Sidi Ifni •
Tan-Tan •

ALGERIA

N ↑

Tarfaya •

El Aaiún •

WESTERN SAHARA

MAURITANIA

ATLANTIC OCEAN

● Capital city
● Major town
▲ Mountain peak
▨ Disputed territory
■ Ancient site

Feet	Meters
16,500	5,000
9,900	3,000
6,600	2,000
3,300	1,000
1,650	500
660	200
0	0

MAP OF MOROCCO

Agadir, B3
Al-Jadida, B2
Anti-Atlas Mountains, B3, C3
Asilah, C1
Atlantic Ocean, A1–A4, B1–B4, C1
Azilal, C3
Azrou, C2

Ben Slimane, C2
Berkane, D1
Berrechid, B2
Bou Arfa, D2
Boujad, C2
Boulemane, C2

Casablanca, B2
Chechaouèn, C1

El Aaiún (disputed territory), A4
El Kelaa des Srarhna, B2
Er Rachidia, C3
Erfoud, C3
Essaouira, B3

Fès, C2
Figuig, D2
Fkih Ben Salah, C2

High Atlas Mountains, B3, C2, C3

Inezgane, B3

Kasba Tadla, C2
Kénitra, C2
Ketama, C1
Khemisset, C2
Khenifra, C2
Khouribga, C2

Larache, C1

Marrakech, B3
Mediterranean Sea, C1, D1
Meknes, C2
Middle Atlas (mountains), C2
Midelt, C2
Mohammedia, B2
Mount Toubkal, B3
Moulouya (river), C2, D1–D2

Ouarzazate, C3
Ouezzane, C1
Oujda, D2
Oum er Rbia, B2, C2

Rif Mountains, C1, C2, D2

Safi, B2
Salé, C2
Sebou (river), C2
Settat, B2
Sidi Bennour, B2
Sidi Ifni, B3
Sidi Slimane, C2
Souk el Arba du Rharb, C2
Sous (river), B3
Strait of Gibraltar, C1

Tangier Peninsula, C1

Tangier, C1
Tan-Tan, A4
Taounate, C2
Taourirt, D2
Tarfaya, A4
Taroudant, B3
Tata, B3
Taza, C2
Tensift (river), B2–B3
Tétouan, C1
Tiznit, B3

Volubilis (ruins), C2

Youssoufia, B2

ECONOMIC MOROCCO

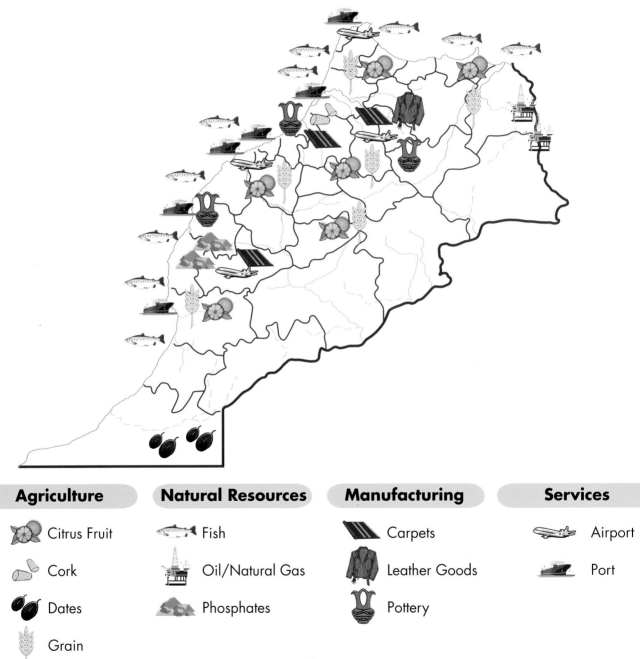

Agriculture	Natural Resources	Manufacturing	Services
Citrus Fruit	Fish	Carpets	Airport
Cork	Oil/Natural Gas	Leather Goods	Port
Dates	Phosphates	Pottery	
Grain			

ABOUT THE ECONOMY

OVERVIEW

After very strong financial growth in the 1990s, Morocco suffered several drought years that slowed its growth. Since 2000, economic growth has not risen above 3.5 percent in any year. Foreign investment is increasing, though capital from abroad often finds bottlenecks in the complex Moroccan bureaucracy. There is also some worry now that Islamic radicalism will make Morocco a less hospitable environment for international business concerns.

GROSS DOMESTIC PRODUCT (GDP)

US$44.5 billion (2003)

GDP BY SECTOR

Agriculture 18 percent, industry 31 percent, services 51 percent

LAND USE

Arable land 10.83 percent, permanent crops 0.83 percent, other 88.34 percent

CURRENCY

1 Moroccan Dirham = 100 centimes
Notes: 10, 20, 50, 100, 200 dirhams
Coins: 1, 5, 10, 20, 50 centimes; 1, 5, 10 dirhams
USD 1 = MAD 9.54 (2005)

INFLATION RATE

1.3 percent (2003)

NATURAL RESOURCES

Phosphorus rock, marine fish, cork and cedar forests, palm groves

MAIN EXPORTS

Clothing and textiles, phosphate products, shellfish and canned fish, citrus and other fruit, tomatoes, cork, rugs, leather goods, pottery

IMPORTS

Crude oil and other fuels, wheat and other cereals, sugar, semifinished products, machinery and IT equipment

MAJOR PORTS

Casablanca, Tangier, Safi, Agadir

TRADE PARTNERS

France, Spain, the United Kingdom, Italy, Germany, United States

WORKFORCE

11.4 million (2003)

WORKFORCE BY OCCUPATION

Agriculture 40 percent, industry 15 percent, services 45 percent

UNEMPLOYMENT RATE

10.7 (2003)

CULTURAL MOROCCO

Volubilis
These well-preserved ruins of a Roman outpost near Meknes attests to the fully developed Roman culture that thrived in Morocco in the pre-Arab era.

American Legation
Morocco was the first country to officially recognize the United States as a country in 1777. The American Legation in Tangier, today a museum, is the first embassy established abroad by the United States.

Fès Medina
This UNESCO world monument is one of the oldest continuously inhabited cities in the world. Bab Boujloud, one of the entrances to this walled city, is decorated in beautiful blue lapis lazuli.

Tour Hassan
This minaret in Rabat is part of an unfinished mosque from the 13th century. The mosque was originally intended to be the largest mosque in the world. It is on the same grounds as the Masouleum of Mohammed V, a beautifully crafted memorial.

Hassan II mosque
The second largest mosque in the world, it is located on the seafront in Casablanca. It was commissioned to commemorate the late King's 60th birthday.

Old Portuguese Fort
The Portuguese once had strongholds up and down the Atlantic coast of Morocco. One of the best preserved is the fort in Essaouira; the seafront fort now houses the shops of woodcarvers, who sell exquisitely worked boxes for which Essaouira is famous.

Stables of Moulay Ismail
These stables, near Meknes, were built by Moulay Ismail to house 12,000 horses. Today only impressive ruins remain.

Djemm al'Fna
This is an open air market, square, and entertainment center in Marrakech. People from all over the world converge to haggle with traders, eat exotic foods, listen to story-tellers, and watch snake charmers and other performers.

Ouarzazate
This town is a gateway to the desert, and the staging post for the filming of many modern desert epics. Nearby are many *qsars* (walled villages) that are centuries old, some of them still inhabited.

ABOUT THE CULTURE

OFFICIAL NAME
Kingdom of Morocco

CAPITAL
Rabat

OTHER MAJOR CITIES
Casablanca, Agadir, Fès, Marrakech, Tangier, Meknès, Oujda.

GOVERNMENT SYSTEM
Constitutional Monarchy

NATIONAL FLAG
A green five-pointed star or pentagram, called the Seal of Sulayman, in the middle of a red flag.

NATIONAL ANTHEM
Hymne Cherifieni

POPULATION
29,891,708 (2004)

POPULATION GROWTH RATE
1.57 percent (2005 estimate)

LIFE EXPECTANCY
68 years (2004)

LITERACY RATE
53% (2003)

ETHNIC GROUPS
Berber, Arab, Jewish, Tuareg

MAJOR RELIGIONS
Muslim 98.7 percent, Christian 1.1 percent, Jewish 0.2 percent

LANGUAGES
Arabic (official), French, Berber dialects

IMPORTANT ANNIVERSARIES
Independence Day (January 11),
Feast of the Throne Day (July 30),
Green March Remembrance Day (November 6)

MAJOR RELIGIOUS FESTIVALS
Muslim New Year, Muharram 1
Aïd es Seghir (end of Ramadan)
Aïd el Kebir
Mouloud (birthday of the Prophet Mohammed)

PROMINENT MOROCCANS
King Mohammed VI, the current monarch
Fatima Mernissi, writer and educator
Hicham El Guerrouj, athlete
Samira Said, singer

TIME LINE

IN MOROCCO	IN THE WORLD
10,000 B.C. Stone-age humans establish primitive pastoral and agricultural systems in Morocco.	
	753 B.C. Rome is founded.
700–600 B.C. Berbers, probably of central Asian origin, are already the dominant ethnic group in Morocco.	
300 B.C. Founding of Volubilis, then capital of the Roman province of Mauritania; now the most extensive Roman ruins in Morocco.	**116–17 B.C.** The Roman Empire reaches its greatest extent, under Emperor Trajan (98–17).
	A.D. 600 Height of Mayan civilization
A.D. 700 Arab invasion; Moulay Idriss founds the first major Muslim dynasty.	**1000** The Chinese perfect gunpowder and begin to use it in warfare.
1100s–1200s Almohad dynasty rules Morocco and present-day Spain and Algeria.	
1259–1550 The Merinid Dynasty rules Morocco, establishing Marrakech as their capital.	**1530** Beginning of trans-Atlantic slave trade organized by the Portuguese in Africa.
	1558–1603 Reign of Elizabeth I of England
	1620 Pilgrims sail the *Mayflower* to America.
1660s First Alaouite Sultan, Moulay Rachid, comes to power in Tafilalet.	**1776** U.S. Declaration of Independence
	1789–99 The French Revolution
1844 Morocco goes to war with France over control of territory.	**1861** The U.S. Civil War begins.
	1869 The Suez Canal is opened.
1912 Morocco becomes a French protectorate under the Treaty of Fès.	**1914** World War I begins.
	1939 World War II begins.

IN MOROCCO	IN THE WORLD
	1945 The United States drops atomic bombs on Hiroshima and Nagasaki.
	1949 The North Atlantic Treaty Organization (NATO) is formed.
1956 French protectorate ends after a nationalist uprising.	
	1957 The Russians launch Sputnik.
1961 King Hassan II comes to power.	
1963 First general elections	
	1966–69 The Chinese Cultural Revolution
1975 King Hassan orders 350,000 civilian volunteers to cross into the Western Sahara. In December Spain withdraws from the territory. Moroccan forces immediately occupy it.	
1976 Moroccan and Algerian troops clash in Western Sahara. Fighting later breaks out between Morocco and Polisario forces.	**1986** Nuclear power disaster at Chernobyl in Ukraine
	1991 Break-up of the Soviet Union
	1997 Hong Kong is returned to China.
1998 Morocco's first opposition-led government comes to power following 1997 elections.	
1999 Death of King Hassan II; coronation of his son Mohammed VI.	**2001** Terrorists crash planes in New York, Washington, D.C., and Pennsylvania.
2003 Forty-one people are killed and many are injured in a series of suicide bomb attacks in Casablanca.	**2003** War in Iraq
2004 King Mohammed V convenes a commission to investigate human rights abuses during his father's reign.	

GLOSSARY

Aïd el Kebir (ah-EED el-kay-BEER)
Muslim festival commemorating Abraham's willingness to sacrifice his son Isaac.

Aïd es Seghir (ah-EED es-say-GEER)
Muslim celebration marking the end of Ramadan.

bilgha (bil-GHAH)
Leather slippers with pointed toes that are open at the back.

djellaba (jel-LAB-uh)
Traditional long outer garment, usually with a hood and worn by both sexes.

fantasia
A display of horsemanship.

hammam (ham-MAM)
Turkish-style public bath.

imam (ee-MAM)
Person who presides over the prayers in Islam.

imdyazn (IM-dee-AZN)
Professional musicians who traveled from village to village singing the news.

Insha'Allah (in-SHAH-lah)
Expression meaning "God willing."

kasbah (KAHS-bah)
A chief's residence, a fortified house, or an entire fortified village.

marabout (MAH-rah-boo)
A saint or holy person.

medersa (may-DER-sah)
Religious boarding school or students' lodging house.

medina (muh-DEE-nah)
The old, medieval part of a city or town, distinct from the French "new town."

moussem (MOO-sem)
Local festival in honor of a *marabout*.

muezzin (MWE-zin)
One who calls the faithful to prayer, usually from the minaret of a mosque.

Ramadan
Muslim month of fasting.

sadaqa (sah-DAK-ah)
Charity, or a special meal offered in memory of someone dead.

Salaam oualeikum (sa-LAAM wa-LAY-koom)
A Muslim greeting meaning "Peace be with you."

souk (sook)
A stall in a market, or a whole market of stalls.

tajine (ta-JEEN)
A traditional pot with a conical lid; also refers to the Moroccan casserole cooked in the same pot.

FURTHER INFORMATION

BOOKS

Graham, R.B. Cunninghame. *Mogreb-El-Acksa: A Journey in Morocco*. Marlboro, VT: Marlboro Press, 1997.

Hargraves, Orin. *Culture Shock! Morocco*. Portland, OR: Graphic Arts Center Publishing Company, 2001.

Kerper, Barrie (editor). *Morocco: An Inspired Anthology and Travel Resource*. New York: Three Rivers Press, 2001.

Maxwell, Gavin. *Lords of the Atlas*. Guilford, Connecticut: Lyons Press, 2001.

Porch, Douglas. *The Conquest of Morocco*. New York: Farrar, Straus and Giroux, 2005.

Rogerson, Barnaby. *A Traveller's History of North Africa*. Northampton, MA: Interlink Publishing Group, 2000.

Wolfert, Paula. *Couscous and Other Good Foods from Morocco*. New York: HarperCollins, 1987.

WEB SITES

Central Intelligence Agency World Factbook (select Morocco from the country list). www.cia.gov/cia/publications/factbook/index.html

Morocco Country Fact Sheet. http://biz.yahoo.com/ifc/ma.html

Morocco Fact File. www.iss.co.za/AF/profiles/Morocco/morocco1.html

Morocco government web site. www.mincom.gov.ma

Statoids: regions of Morocco. www.statoids.com/uma.html

USAID: Morocco Country Fact Sheet. www.usaid.gov/pubs/cbj2002/ane/ma/

VIDEOS

Morocco: Marrakesh. DVD. City Hall Records, 2005.

MUSIC

Apocalypse Across the Sky. Master Musicians Of Jajouka. Axiom / Pgd, 1992.

Immigri. Mara & Jamal. Barraka, 1997.

Jardin Andalou. Sapho. Celluloid (Melodie), 1997.

Songs & Rhythms of Morocco. Various artistes. Lyrichord Discs Inc., 1997.

Traditional Music and Songs. Nass El Ghiwan. Buda Musique, 1995.

Under the Moroccan Sky. Various artistes. Sounds True Direct, 2001.

Voice of the Atlas. Najat Aatabou. Globe Style, 1995.

BIBLIOGRAPHY

Bowles, Paul. *Morocco*. New York: Harry N. Abrams, 1993.

Gumley, Frances. *The Pillars of Islam: An Introduction to the Islamic Faith*. London: BBC Books, 1990.

Lerner Publications. *Morocco—In Pictures*. Minneapolis, MN: Lerner Publications, 1989.

Mernissi, Fatima. *Doing Daily Battle: Interviews with Moroccan Women*. Rutgers, NJ: Rutgers University Press, 1989.

Nelson, Harold D. (editor). *Morocco, A Country Study*. Washington, D.C.: U.S. Government Printing Office, 1986.

Wilkins, Frances. *Morocco*. New York: Chelsea House, 1988.

INDEX

Abraham, 116, 125

Africa, 8, 9, 14, 16, 17, 19, 21, 25, 45, 57, 58, 59, 60, 61, 62, 64, 69, 81, 88, 93, 95, 102

agriculture, 8, 13, 19, 37, 38, 39, 40–41, 50, 54, 61, 109, 121
    dairy products, 39, 40
    fruit, 14, 20, 41, 121
    grain, 13, 14, 20, 39, 121
    irrigation, 13, 28, 38, 40, 41
    olives, 37, 53, 54, 121
    vegetables, 14, 40, 119, 121

Alaouites, 22, 23, 24, 31

Algeria, 7, 8, 9, 10, 16, 24, 26, 31, 39, 57, 59, 60, 61, 62, 94, 96

Almohads, 22, 23

Almoravids, 22

Andalous Mosque, 91

Andalusian garden, 103

animals,
    antelope, 14, 15, 19
    Barbary apes, 15
    Berber skink, 15
    bubal hartebeest, 14
    camels, 15, 45, 61
    chameleons, 15
    desert hedgehog, 15
    elephants, 14
    gazelle, 15, 19, 126
    giraffes, 19

    goats, 11, 15, 55, 105, 121
    jerboa, 15
    Red foxes, 15
    sheep, 11, 15, 47, 105, 116, 121
    Wild boar, 15
    zebras, 19

Arabs, the, 3, 16, 23, 24, 27, 57, 58, 61, 62, 63, 64, 65, 81, 84, 90, 91, 100, 107, 121
    Arab culture, 19, 63, 64, 70, 78, 90, 91, 93, 97, 99, 100, 106

architecture, 35, 88, 89, 91, 99, 100, 102, 103

Atlantic coast, 7, 10, 11, 12, 13, 14, 16, 25

Atlantic Ocean, 7, 8, 10, 44, 54, 62, 89

Bab el Mansour, 103
Belgium, 59
Benzekri, Driss, 33
Berbers, 7, 19, 20, 22, 23, 24, 27, 57, 58, 60, 60–61, 61, 62, 63, 64, 65, 72, 73, 78, 81, 84, 85, 90, 93, 95, 97, 100, 104, 105, 106, 107, 109, 115, 121, 125
Byzantine Empire, 21

caids, 31
Carthage, 20
Carthaginians, 19, 20, 25, 60
Chamber of Counselors, 32
Chamber of Representatives, 32
cities and towns, 3, 7, 10, 11, 14, 16, 17, 20, 21, 22, 25, 26, 27, 35, 42, 43, 44, 52, 55, 58, 61, 63, 65, 68, 69, 70, 71, 72, 73, 75, 77, 78, 81, 84, 88, 90, 91, 96, 102, 103, 107, 109, 110, 113, 118
  Agadir, 10, 17, 41, 44, 59
  Al-Jadida, 10
  Al Hoceima, 10, 26
  Asilah, 10
  Casablanca, 10, 11, 13, 16, 17, 24, 33, 42, 44, 47, 55, 58, 69, 84, 86, 88, 113
  Ceuta, 7, 9, 47
  El Aaiún, 75
  Erfoud, 11
  Er Rachidia, 11
  Essaouira, 10
  Fès, 11, 16, 17, 22, 25, 31, 43, 63, 75, 83, 90, 91, 93, 105, 107, 113, 124
  Fès el Bali, 91
  Imilchil, 119
  Kénitra, 10, 113
  Ketama, 13
  Marrakech, 11, 16, 17, 22, 23, 34, 46, 52, 59, 69, 87, 100, 105, 106, 111, 124, 125
  Meknès, 16, 17, 22, 103, 105, 107, 113, 119
  Melila, 9
  Merzouga, 7, 11
  Mohammedia, 10
  Moulay Idriss, 81
  Ouarzazate, 11, 13, 104
  Oujda, 10, 16, 17, 58, 59
  Rabat, 11, 14, 16, 17, 19, 22, 35, 55, 58, 69, 102, 103, 104, 113, 125
  Rio d'Oro, 7, 9
  Safi, 10, 17
  Sidi Ifni, 25, 26
  Tangier, 7, 9, 10, 13, 17, 21, 25, 69, 107, 113
  Tarfaya, 26
  Taroudant, 11
  Taza, 61
  Tétouan, 10, 17, 124
climate, 12, 14, 19, 37, 39, 121
  rainfall, 13, 14, 37, 50, 51, 68
  temperature, 12, 13, 14

desert, 7, 11, 12, 14, 15, 22, 44, 45, 50, 61, 69, 72, 102, 121
  Sahara Desert, 8, 11, 13, 17, 19, 26, 50, 63, 95, 102, 121
diffa, 110, 128
Djemm el'Fna, 106, 111, 121

economy, 10, 13, 25, 37, 38, 39, 40, 41, 42, 44, 46, 47, 51, 53, 54, 58, 74, 88, 96, 97, 99, 109, 112
  industry, 28, 37, 42, 43
  informal sector, 37, 46–47, 73
  leather goods, 39, 43, 104, 105
  oil and electricity, 11, 37, 39, 40, 42, 50, 54, 109
  phosphates, 11, 29, 37, 39, 42, 54
  textiles, 39, 43
  tourism, 10, 37, 39, 44, 45, 55, 86, 96, 109, 113, 118, 119
  unemployment, 33, 38, 61
education, 26, 31, 33, 34, 38, 58, 73, 75, 76, 78, 96
El Mansour mosque, 87
emigration, 17
Europe, 7, 23, 24, 25, 31, 34, 35, 37, 40, 41, 44, 47, 54, 58, 60, 78, 84, 96, 97, 113
  Europeans, 10, 24, 25, 57
European Union, 35, 37

food and beverages,
  b'stilla, 94, 124, 125, 127
  briouat, 126
  Café cassé, 127
  Café Ras el Hanout, 127
  couscous, 123, 125, 126, 128
  harira, 83
  keneffa, 125
  ktaif, 126
  mechoui, 125
  mint tea, 67, 110, 122, 128, 129
  Ras el Hanout, 127
  sharbat, 127
  shebbakia, 83
  tajine, 122, 123, 125, 128
  warka, 124, 126
France, 21, 22, 25, 26, 37, 59, 75
  French, the, 17, 24, 25, 26, 27, 28, 31, 35, 57, 65, 71, 77, 91, 93, 96, 103, 121, 124, 127

General Lyautey, 26, 27, 71
Germany, 25, 37, 59
Gibraltar, 7, 9
Goths, 21
Great Britain, 9, 25, 37
  British, the, 25, 67, 121
Great Mosque, 88
Green March, the, 29, 115

handicrafts, 99, 104–105
  bilgha, 105
  hands of Fatima, 105
  kilim, 104
Hassan II, 27, 28, 34, 50, 86, 88, 113
Hassan II Mosque, 86, 88–89
healthcare, 28, 33, 38, 65, 74, 75

Idriss, Moulay, 22, 81, 90, 119
Idriss the II, Moulay, 91
infant mortality, 74
International Court of Justice, 29
International Labor Organization, 73
International Monetary Fund, 38
Islam, 21, 22, 27, 31, 33, 34, 35, 57, 59, 60, 61, 62, 63, 75, 77, 81, 82, 83, 84, 85, 86, 88, 89, 90, 91, 93, 100, 101, 103, 116, 117, 118, 129
  fundamentalism, 35, 84
  imam, 86
  Islamic calendar, 117
  Koran, 63, 82, 84, 86, 89, 93, 94, 101, 105
  medersas, 81, 86, 87, 88, 100
  muezzins, 82, 86, 106
  Prophet Mohammed, 23, 34, 62, 64, 81, 105, 116
  Ramadan, 82, 83, 91, 116, 117, 125
  zaouias, 87, 91
Ismail, Moulay, 17, 22, 23, 24

Istiqlal Party, 27
Italy, 25, 37, 59

Jews, 58, 93

Karaouiyine Mosque, 91
kasbahs, 17, 72, 102
koubba, 85, 87, 118

languages,
    Arabic, 31, 42, 60, 61, 62, 64, 65,
        93, 94, 95, 96, 97, 101, 106, 129
    Chleuh, 95
    Darija, 94
    English, 96
    French, 26, 57, 93, 96, 97
    Spanish, 42, 96
    Tamazight, 95
    Tarafit, 95
Libya, 39, 59, 60
life expectancy, 74

Madagascar, 27
Maghreb countries, 31, 62, 101
marabout, 85, 118, 119
marriage, 76, 77, 107, 115, 119, 128
    polygamy, 77
Mecca, 82, 83, 86, 88, 117
mechouar, 35
medina, 27, 70, 71, 73, 77, 85, 91, 99,
    110, 111
Mediterranean coast, 7, 8, 9, 10, 13,
    44, 96
Mediterranean Sea, 7, 8, 10, 54
minimum wage, 73
Mohammed V, 27, 28, 31, 34, 35
Mohammed VI, 17, 29, 31, 33, 34, 115
monarchy, 28, 31, 32, 33, 34–35, 64
Moors, 57, 100, 102, 107
mountains, 3, 7, 8, 9, 14, 16, 17, 20, 44,
    63, 65, 69, 72, 96
    Anti-Atlas, 8, 13, 61, 95
    High Atlas, 8, 9, 11, 12, 13, 17, 60,
        95, 104, 115, 119
    Middle Atlas, 8, 11, 13, 14, 16, 20,
        95, 104, 124
    Rif, 7, 8, 11, 12, 13, 16, 20, 22, 95,
        96
    Toubkal, 9
moussem, 111, 115, 116, 118–119
music, 97, 99, 106–107, 109, 111, 115
    chaabi, 106
    imdyazn, 107

rai, 106

national dress,
    djellabas, 70, 79
    kaftans, 79
national flag, 35
national holidays,
    Allegiance Day, 115
    Festival of the Throne, 115
    Green March Remembrance Day,
        115
    Independence Day, 115
    Labor Day, 115
    New Year's Day, 84, 115
    Revolution of the King and the Peo-
        ple, 115
Netherlands, 59
nomadic people, 11, 61, 63, 72, 109
North Africa, 8, 9, 14, 16, 17, 19, 21, 45,
    57, 60, 61, 62, 69, 81, 93, 95

Oqba ben Nafi, 62, 81

parliament, 31, 32, 33
pashas, 31
Phoenicians, 19, 20, 25, 60, 121
pisé, 72
plants, 14–15
    cacti, 15
    cedar, 14, 15, 100
    eucalyptus, 14
    oak, 14, 100
    pine, 100, 127
    thistles, 15
Polisario Front, 29, 32
pollution, 52, 54, 55
    air pollution, 52
    litter, 55
    water pollution, 54, 55
Portugal, 24, 25, 42
pre-Sahara, 7, 12, 13
Protectorate, 25, 26, 27, 35, 71, 93,
    96, 109

Rabat man, 19
recipes,
    Halib B-Looz, 131
    Maaqoda, 130
recycling, 55
religious holidays,
    Aïd el Kebir, 116, 117, 125
    Aïd es Seghir, 116, 118
    Aïd Mouloud, 116

Muharram, 116
rivers, 8, 21, 90, 91
    Moulouya, 8
    Sebou, 8
    Sous, 59
Roman Empire, the, 9, 14, 19, 20, 21,
    81
    Romans, the, 19, 20, 21, 25, 61

Saadians, 23
sadaqa, 129
Sahrawi Arab Democratic Republic,
    28, 29
souks, 46, 70, 71, 85, 104, 124
Spain, 3, 7, 9, 17, 21, 24, 25, 26, 29, 31,
    37, 42, 47, 59, 64, 90, 93, 96, 100,
    102, 103, 107, 121
    Andalusian culture, 90, 99, 100,
        107, 121
    Iberians, 64
sport, 15, 44, 109, 112, 113
    golf, 44, 109, 112, 113
    hunting, 14, 15, 109, 112
    skiing, 44, 113
    soccer, 109, 112, 113
    water sports, 109, 112, 113
Strait of Gibraltar, 7, 25
Sultan Hafid, 25

terrorism, 33, 44, 84
Treaty of Fès, 25
Tunisia, 20, 21, 31, 60, 62, 74, 90, 94,
    100

United Nations, 29, 32
United States, 5, 37, 41, 113

Vandals, 21
Versailles, 22
Volubilis, 14, 19, 20, 21, 81

water scarcity, 20, 39, 40, 41, 50–51,
    53
Western Sahara, 7, 11, 28, 29, 31, 32, 38,
    58, 74, 75, 115
women, 32, 33, 59, 60, 68, 70, 72, 73, 75,
    76, 77, 78, 79, 85, 86, 88, 103, 105,
    107, 110, 111, 115, 119
World Bank, 38

Yacoub el Mansour, 22

zaouia, 87, 91

144